The Eyes of the Blind

WALTER C. LANYON

Published by
Union Life Ministries
1977

ISBN # 1-889870-06-4

PUBLISHER'S PREFACE

What we call the Union Life message of Oneness in Christ, Paul called, "the mystery which has been hidden from the past ages and generations; but now has been manifested to His saints" (Col. 1:26). This mystery, of "Christ in us, our hope of glory", is available to all believers. Men need no longer die in a wilderness of separation, struggle and defeat. There *is* "a Sabbath rest for the people of God" (Heb. 4:9). Since Pentecost, the reality of full heirship—co-crucifixion, co-resurrection, and co-ascension in Christ—is readily available to all who will acknowledge that the Kingdom of God is within them. "The one who joins himself to the Lord is one spirit with Him" (1 Cor. 6:17).

No twentieth century author has proclaimed the truth of Oneness any more clearly and eloquently than Walter C. Lanyon. Yet the bulk of his books are no longer available. Therefore, UNION LIFE MINISTRIES is republishing a few of Lanyon's out-of-print books to make his writings available once again.

However, a word of explanation is in order. Since Lanyon wrote primarily to mature Christians who have begun to see with a "single eye", he leaves "the elementary teachings about the Christ . . . not laying again a foundation of repentance from dead works and faith toward God" (Heb. 6:1). Instead of seeing some as little children and young men, he writes as if all readers are "fathers" (1 John 2:13).

Lanyon's writings make only passing reference to sin, to the Lord Jesus' unique Diety in His incarnation as "God manifest in the flesh", to our identification with Him in His substitutionary death, and to other such fundamental truths. His limited emphasis on the foundations of faith in Christ is his way of pressing readers on to further reaches of maturity, not a denial of any foundational truths.

We in UNION LIFE MINISTRIES most certainly believe that, "Whoever denies the Son does not have the Father" (1 John 2:23); "and there is salvation in no one else; for there is no name under heaven that has been given among men, by which we must be saved" (Acts 4:12).

But we also agree with Paul (and with Lanyon) when Paul says, "Therefore from now on we recognize no man according to the flesh; even though we have known Christ according to the flesh, yet now we know Him thus no longer" (2 Cor. 5:16). In maturity, the day finally comes when the substance (the Spirit) swallows up the shadow and the symbol (the historical and the material). As spirit persons, we must not avoid the metaphysical (beyond the physical) dimension, which is the ultimate true reality. "Beware that you do not lose the substance by grasping at the shadow" (Aesop).

Few writers take us into this wonderful dimension of living which Paul labels as "the heavenly places" (Eph. 1:3,20). Lanyon is one of the few who writes of life in that dimension, where we "do not judge according to appearance, but judge with righteous judgment" (John 7:24). We need not always be caught up in a two-power conflict, but with a single eye see the One "who works all things (good *and* evil) after the counsel of His will" (Eph. 1:11).

So do not look for typical, foundational Biblical truths in this book. Lanyon only seeks to be a confirming witness to ultimate truths, such as total adequacy and complete victory in the Eternal Now of our Oneness with the Father. **Be prepared to see with a single eye, and your whole body will be marvelously flooded with inextinguishable light.**

UNION
LIFE
MINISTRIES

UNION LIFE MINISTRIES has a bi-monthly magazine which emphasizes the liberating truths of our union with Christ. It is available without charge. Write to:
UNION LIFE MINISTRIES
P.O. Box 2877
Glen Ellyn, IL 60137
Telephone (312) 469 7757.

CONTENTS

The Eyes
of the
Blind

THE EYES OF THE BLIND

"THEN SHALL the eyes of the blind be opened, and the ears of the deaf unstopped."

Have you ever thought what it must be like to have been blind—physically speaking—and then suddenly to have your sight restored? The wonders of a universe in which you have lived and only contacted by touching, smelling and hearing, are suddenly all transformed by sight. A whole new universe lies before you with colour, beauty, form and outline, and yet it would be the identical universe in which you had been living all the time. Everything that you were experiencing with the re-gained sight had always been there, and instantly available to you, but you did not see it—and even if you knew it, you did not experience the "feel" of seeing it. It is one thing to write about a field of flowers and make that writing real and living, but it is another to suddenly find yourself in the midst of such a field, knee-deep in beauty and drenched with the glory of the living, pulsating expression of life. Can you imagine the thousand and one revelations that would take place in coming from blindness into light? Blessings as infinite as the sands of the sea would be yours.

11

Can you imagine the joy of hearing your first symphony after having seen—as far as you were concerned—a soundless orchestra sway a vast number of people? It would be too wonderful for words—so full of revelation.—The joy of untwining the various strands of music that wove themselves into a glorious melody. And yet you would have to admit it had all existed all the time, but you did not hear it.

A man who had been blind would not change anything by regaining his sight, and yet everything would be changed. He would experience the process of having been suddenly forced into a new universe, and yet he would remain where he had always been. It is wonderful!

And so the blind one is told of the beauties of Nature and the universe. He finally knows all about it, but it still only exists in the mental part of his make-up, because he does not *experience* it. Until you experience a thing yourself, it is only in the realm of the mental or on the plane of imagination, and until it is brought out into actual experience, it is of no practical value to you.

For forty years the Children of Israel roamed across a desert which might have been traversed in a few weeks—but it took them forty years to SEE—or experience—the promised land, flowing with milk and honey.

When Jesus said the Kingdom of Heaven is at hand, he stated a clear, concise and absolute fact. Many believed it mentally, but to see it physically seemed another thing.

The vision of the "double eye" is never true. Seeing with the eye of Spirit the perfect realm of harmony and expression, and with the eye of matter, a shifting, changing, chaotic world, results in a terrible mirage. Battling against these false laws and trying to offset them with the Divine is a tiresome and fruitless proposition.

It takes something bigger than argument to open the blind eyes. It takes Reality. It takes "Recognition" and "acceptance of" that which is. "When thine eye is single thy whole body is full of light." By the Recognition of the *Presence* Here and Now, you will see the veils rent before your eyes, and behold the perfect manifestation. And you will discover these veils, which you have rent by the Absolute Acceptance, are nothing but thin gossamer of human belief, upon which are painted the life history of a human being—birth, growth, tragedy, sickness, unhappiness, decay, and death.

As "there is nothing to be destroyed in all My Holy Mountain," then something must be *restored* to its rightful place. The distorted vision that is seeing all sorts of evil is properly aligned, "When thine eye becomes single thy whole body is full of Light."

The dual nature of man (the prodigal feeding with the swine and the beloved Son seated at a sumptuous banquet) must be wiped out. Jesus Christ has to be Recognised as One, instead of two. The "twain shall be one." The body, or physical nature of man which is all that has ever suffered, sinned and experienced evil, has to be made one with the Soul, which has known all the glorious freedom of a Prince of the Realm, a Son of the Living God, upon whom all the heavenly gifts have been bestowed.

Too long have we kept these apart. Too long have

we been trying to use this Spiritual side of our nature to heal the physical—like rubbing on a salve or ointment. The Light of understanding is breaking through the veils of darkness that have divided man from his Soul, and he is beginning to experience the "Word made flesh" as a reality.

"Son of the Living God, joint heir with Christ, partaker in this glorious universe of all good, arise and shine, for thy light has come and the glory of God has risen upon thee."

"That which God hath joined together let no man put asunder," is the marriage of Spirit. It is the union of man and his Soul. It is the materialization of Spirit and the spiritualization of matter. It is the union of Jesus the carpenter with the Christ the Son of God, evolving therefrom the glorious Jesus-Christ. It is exactly what the human side of you has been looking for all these centuries. It is the one thing that will again lead you, not only to the portals, but through the gates into the very Garden of Eden, which you left when you separated yourself from your soul.

"Then shall the eyes of the blind be opened and the ears of the deaf unstopped."

Do you begin to see? You who read these lines. It is not anything you can learn—it is something that *is being given you* for the mere acceptance; for the mere Recognition of the Presence. Are you afraid of it? It is so immense, and it will suddenly cause you to experience all the things that you have tried for years to demonstrate, and have failed; yea, and even more—it will show you the things "that eyes have not seen and ears have not heard, and that have not entered into the heart of man." "Only believe," and the answer of the dual nature comes, "Yea, Lord, I believe, help Thou mine unbelief." For the moment you have Recognized this Presence, there will be no further request of "help Thou mine unbelief," for such a thing could not exist. There is no room for it in the consciousness that became full of the Recognition of the Presence Here and Now. You can perform this miracle for yourself, and see the "word made flesh." You can experience the glorious Marriage with the Lamb—the marriage with your soul; the oneness with your God-self. It is wonderful! There is no Royal Road to this attainment, because it is so simple and natural for the Son to return to the Father, yea, in spite of all his shortcomings, weaknesses, and failures. No one can do it for you. You will stop trying to get them to, when your eyes are opened and your ears are unstopped. This will come to pass *just* as soon as you listen to the "Still small voice" in yourself. Just as soon as you listen to the Voice of Christ within you, and stop trying to take someone else's *advice* about your return to the Father, you will find you have arrived. You have such understanding that you can operate the promises and experience the joys of them all Here and Now.

"Claim your right and press your claim" as the son of the Living God—accept your God-given heritage, because now you have Recognized your one-ness— soul and body are one, and you are ready and able to partake of the heavenly manna. "Be whole" was said for this express purpose. You can never be whole until this perfect union of body and soul takes place

within you, and it takes place the moment you Recognize the Presence.

The heavenly manna might fall down all about you, but until you were made of such substance as could partake of the heavenly manna, you could not taste it. Just as the physically blind man moves daily in a world of light and colour, and knows virtually nothing of it. For him it does not exist, or it exists only in mind.

For many Truth students this glorious Kingdom of Heaven only exists in mind. It is something they are going to demonstrate, make appear—or create out of concentration or thought processes—yet the years go by and they come no nearer the ultimate goal than they did in the most orthodox teaching. "I came a light into this world—to light every man unto salvation." That in this mental darkness in which we have been standing, this glorious "I" of Spirit, in the midst of each one of us, has come a Light unto this world—to light every man unto salvation. The salvation from the human darkness and the mental wilderness of words and beliefs.

"The former things have passed away"—yes, even the former heaven and earth—concepts of spirit and matter—are passing away, and in their place is the lovely new heaven and earth, something concrete and real, here and now for you to experience and live in. And it has been *here* all the time, though you only now see it "descending out of the clouds" of your beliefs. You are spirit materialized and matter spiritualized, and so you are able to experience the new rate of vibration, or law, that enables you to understand things that formerly you hardly imagined existed.

Dare you, who read this line, believe in yourself—your God-self? Have you the *courage* to accept your good? You do not have to go out and tell the world, you do not have to become excited. "I come silently, as a thief in the night"—but you must put a seal upon your lips, and be the new "whole-man"—the perfect being of spiritualized matter and materialized spirit. Be still. "See that you tell no man"—you will know whether it be of the Spirit or not. "Prove me and see." You will know because a wonderful common-sense basis of life will come to you, and the temple will be cleansed of a lot of mental debris—theories, teachings and beliefs.

Either every one of the promises of the Bible are true or none of them are. What do you think? I said *you!* not someone else. What do *you* think? Are they? and if they are—what are you going to do about it? Many people have mistaken emotion, excitement and all sorts of strange things, as signs of the coming of Spirit. It is as glorious and free from all this foolishness as the coming of dawn. And you can accept the word of the Master and have the "scales drop from off your eyes," and see your glorious universe as it is, and not as it seemed to be through the blind eyes.

"The moment this Truth is Recognized it will make itself manifest." The moment you—I am speaking to you the reader—Recognize the Presence it makes itself manifest. It is wonderful!

"The spirit of the Presence of the consciousness of

God fills all space, no place is vacant of the fulness thereof."

"Though God may not be visible to you, I AM always with you. I have established this Truth, and with or without a body, it is operative. It is even more operative when you do not see Me. Nothing can stop the operation of this Truth, for I have established it."

Are you beginning to see that this glorious Impersonal Life lies within the immediate range of your attainment? You have fed long enough on the husks of human teaching. The spirit of the message is between the lines. The spirit of the lecture is that which is not said—then why discuss words and theories about the Truth? Do you see? And yet this does not make it necessary for you to stop anyone who wants to continue to seek among the husks of material teaching. You have to "Arise and go to your Father" by yourself—and there will be no need of props and helps. You have the new vision that will carry you straight through all the human beliefs that yet confront you. Do not try to make this journey with another. There is so much that the Father has to say to you. Impersonal Life is the most personal life in the world—because you begin at last to see a reason *to be.*

"Then shall the eyes of the blind be opened and the ears of the deaf unstopped." Beloved! that day has arrived for you, and in the deep secret place of this Recognition you are finding it for yourself, and are going on into your glorious expression with sealed lips. Lips that are sealed in the right way, are opened so that the God Voice can utter its song of

Joy which will heal the Nations. And the unstopped ears shall be unstopped to the inflow of God language which no man has uttered, because there are no words to express such a wonderful Revelation. No wonder the command: "Be still and know that I AM God." This I AM in the midst of you will speak to you a new language now that the ears are unstopped. That which stopped the ears was the clogged-up material beliefs in a double universe. Do you hear? Do you begin to see that the new message, which will come to you through the unstopped ears, will be that of attainment and self-expression? The ways and means with which to accomplish this will be there, as if you suddenly by a new sense "felt" your way into a new state; "sensed" your way, into a new state. Yes, something like that. It is wonderful!

OPEN–YE GATES OF DAWN

"Open!"

The glorious resonance of the Voice reverberates to the uttermost part of the Golden City and awakens the Keeper of the Gates.

"Open!"

The echo of the word sends it again forth on its mission of awakening.

"Open—ye Gates of Dawn."

The glorious gates of the new Day, into which you are about to enter, are swinging open to you. The flooding light of revelation, of joy, is coming out to you and bearing you up into a place of understanding.

"Son of Man, pass through."

At last your pass-word has been heard and you are allowed to enter the place of Attainment. You have arrived at the point of manifestation, "The Word shall become flesh." The Spiritualization of matter and the Materialization of Spirit. You have at last awakened from the long night of dreaming about an imaginary heaven to which you were going, or which you were going to demonstrate. You have awakened to find yourself already entering the Gates of this State of Consciousness.

"Then cometh the end when he shall have delivered up the Kingdom of God, even the Father, when he shall have put down all rule and all authority and power."

The time comes when the end of the human believing that the Kingdom is going to be made manifest in some future day has come, and the Kingdom stands revealed, and all rule, power and authority, other than God-power, is put down.

"As we have borne the image of the earthly, we shall also bear the image of the heavenly."

Do you note there is no speculation about this statement? It does not say *maybe, perhaps* or *perchance*. It says "As surely as you have borne the image of the earthly, just so *surely* shall you bear the image of the heavenly." Do you begin to see why Jesus admired the Centurion? There was fearless authority about him. He knew that he had authority in material things and he recognized that Jesus had authority in things spiritual. Do you begin to understand how the "weak knees" must be strengthened? You must learn to assert your God-given heritage and accept that which belongs to you.

"Arise and shine"—you have to do it for yourself, nobody else however strong is going to rise for you. Do you begin to see the finality of the statements of this power?

"Rise, gird on your armour" does not mean you are going to fight, but that you are going to "speak with authority"; that you have come to the place where all the power of supposed spirituality is done away with, in favour of the meekness of Recognition which Jesus used. The meekness of Might. Might that knows itself need not parade in the Streets of the World to curry favours.

"Ye shall decree a thing and it shall come to pass." There it stands firmer than the rock of Gibraltar. "Not one jot or tittle" shall be given up until it is all fulfilled. Do you see the power of Recognition? Do you see that this true self is just the opposite of this false personality that has been spreading itself and its pigmy accomplishments, like a peacock? Authority is shown only because it is necessary to dissolve human belief. Can you see what the Spirit is saying to us—yes, to you as you read, and to me as I write? It is actually urging us to accept the glorious Power of the Sons of the Living God. No matter what the seeming belief is at the moment, its day is done because the light that is flooding in on us will make its nothingness apparent.

"Behold I show you the mysteries. We shall not all sleep, but we shall all be changed." Do you hear the finality of that statement? It says that "we shall not all sleep"—think it over. Aren't you glad for the deep-hidden things of spirit that are being revealed to us? We will make agreement on many of them—you as you read and I as I write. We shall tell each other of it when we come along the "Highway of Wholeness."

The suddenness of this revelation or manifestation is made apparent in:

"In a moment (maybe while you are reading) in the twinkling of any eye ... all shall be changed." No wonder we are glad, and no wonder we have stopped trying to tell the other man what to do, and what not to do, and have gone in for the deep underlying truth which will reveal itself to us in concrete manifestation.

"But the manifestation of the Spirit is given to every man to profit withal." Do not be afraid any more. "If ye be in the spirit ye are no more under the curse of the law" of human belief. And the Manifestation of the Spirit is given to every man so that he may in turn have the substance of life.

The belief in sickness, no matter what its duration, is wiped out when you contemplate this wonderful fact:

"God has set the members every one of them in the body, as it hath pleased Him."

Do you suppose it pleased God to "set a member" of the body in perfection and have it eaten away with disease? Do you suppose you would deliberately let *your* child be destroyed inch by inch before your eyes?

Well, think it over. If God has "set the members" of our bodies they must be, and are, set in perfection, and this undeniable Truth is so everlastingly right that not ten thousand years of human belief can offset it. And not ten thousand years of human learning can move it. And not ten thousand years of human power can go against this glorious established Fact. "God hath set the members, every one of them in the body, as it pleased him." Nothing is going to change that fact, no matter what you have seen or accepted about the body, and just as soon as you see this incontrovertible fact, you will suddenly loose the mist-i-fication of human belief that is picturing inharmony or dislocation of any member of your body. Isn't it wonderful! Aren't you glad we are having this wonderful Revelation? "Having done all we will stand and see."

"I thank my God (the God within my consciousness) always on your behalf. For the grace of God which is given you by Jesus Christ." Recognizing and thanking God in the midst of our consciousness and Recognizing the God in another, operating the glorious power of Grace, which neutralizes all the human beliefs, is the natural expression of the Son of the Living God.

"*Because* the foolishness of God is wiser than men; and the weakness of God is stronger than men." *Because* this God power is above any man-made doctrine or creed; *because* the power of God makes all human power appear as weakness, *because* of all this, do you rejoice in your God-given heritage.

"The hidden wisdom which God ordained before the world unto our glory," that same is now being revealed to us. It is something that has not been written or spoken by man. It is that which is revealed to you, Oh Singing Heart—it is being revealed to you, in the secret place of the Most High. Right Now.

This glorious wisdom is being revealed by the Spirit—the hidden things are being given to you by the "sense" that is not listed among the five warring human senses. "God hath revealed them unto us by His Spirit, for the Spirit searcheth all things, yea, the deep hidden things of God." It is wonderful!

"For the kingdom of God is not in words but in power." The avalanche of words has passed away and the revelation of the Kingdom that is Power, is made manifest. The Kingdom that is more than imagination —the Kingdom that is power and full of glorious manifestation is here and now.

"These things have I spoken to you in proverbs; but the time cometh when I shall no more speak unto you in proverbs, but I shall shew you plainly of the Father." It is so written.

*   *   *   *   *

And so I stand on the terrace of the Castle, "Shining Lakes" which Spirit has provided as a place, where this message should be given, and written to *you*, and look out across the glorious park, in the valley. It is like a great pit of flames, so gorgeous are the autumn colourings; and beyond lie the shining lakes—like great burnished mirrors in the evening sun.

"The Heavens declare the glory of Him who made all things. Each day repeats the story. Each night some tribute brings."

Night closes in, as silently as light comes and goes. The starry space about me enfolds me; out of the lake comes the red-gold moon, suddenly lighting the surface until it appears to be on fire.

In the distance comes a rumbling—it sounds like the noise of something running down. It is the old wheel of time beginning to use up what little energy it has left. Materialism is running down. It is worn out. It has used up its inheritance. The monotonous old pattern repeated over and over is worn out. "There is nothing new under the sun." Nothing very alarming or disheartening about that, although it does show up the futility of the human régime, but when you think that the sun only shines on a very little spot in the Great Universe, Hope rises high to know that which, figuratively speaking, is on the other side of the little sun.

It is this sudden realization that God is beyond all the little symbols of this earth, that causes us to pause for a moment and contemplate something that can and will break the stupid treadmill of existence. It is wonderful! From the Soul of Me comes the song—"Open—Open—Open, ye Gates of Dawn—the Son of Man, pass through." I am singing it to you and to myself and to the whole universe, and yet I seem to be silent. I am singing it in the way you can best hear and you will join in with me—in the silent, singing, joyous command—"Open—Open—Open, ye Gates of Dawn"; this will open up a new field of illumination to you. The gates of *your dawn* of the New Day of which we have been talking. Presently the earth manifestation which seems to be silent will be quickened to the tempo of the new dimension and will sing in perfect unison with its soul, "Open, open, open—ye gates of Dawn." The glorious flooding light is even now breaking on the horizon. It is *your* new day—with new and glorious expressions awaiting you. You have at last released yourself from the old wheel of Fate, and are thrown off into the glorious reality of Life that is not cast in a hard fast mold, but which is caught and held in the Chalice of Inspiration—in the Holy Grail of your Soul. "There shall be no night there." The old idea of problems being necessary to the unfoldment of man shall have been defeated finally, and man shall walk untrammelled and free.

"For I AM a Man (i-festation) in Authority, and I say to this servant (idea) 'go' (into fulfilment) and he goeth, and to another 'come' and he cometh." The I AM in you that is rising into its place of power by reason of this glorious process of Recognition has "healing in his wings" for all your misunderstanding of life. The little pigmy personality that tried so hard

to do things and make things happen has given place
to the glorious Being of Light that is ever at the point
of Attainment. "Let not the right hand know what
the left hand doeth," pertains to your spiritual work.
You cannot have the blessing as long as you are standing before the world and listing the marvellous
things you have done for God. Without you, God
would manage to get along somehow.

A little dog running down the street with a tin can
attached to his tail, is in reality creating everything
from which he is running. So is it with man. "The
wicked—and we are all wicked as long as we believe
in two powers—fleeth when no man pursueth." Do
you see why all the flurrying around on the outside is
not going to enable you to set aside the condition?
You are (however bitter this may seem) creating the
condition from which you are suffering. Isn't it wonderful—and do you see why we are told to be still?
The moment the dog that is so terrified at the noise is
still, the noise is also still. The moment you are still,
the glorious soul of you will silence all the human
clamouring and fear.

"It is your Father's good pleasure." Do you hear?
It says "It is YOUR Father's good pleasure to give you
the Kingdom." Who is your Father? Is He a some-
what glorified prototype of your human father? Then
if so, he takes on the limitations of your human father,
but when you learn to call no MAN—not any human
MAN—your father, but one which is in heaven—then
do you see that it is possible for *your* Father to give
YOU the Kingdom of Heaven. It is wonderful! Are
you afraid to take it?

What is the matter, have you stumbled and fallen

down? Are you, too, deep in the mire of human thought? Does someone else who is a spiritual authority say you cannot Speak the Word of Christ? Beloved! you are greater than all of these—no matter what their names may be—the moment you Recognize the Presence, and the Gates of Hell shall not prevail against you. Do you hear? The moment you rise to this Recognition the evaporation of these beliefs takes place and in the place of cursing comes blessing. "Every tongue that is incensed against thee shall be put to shame"—every human belief shall be destroyed —and the former things shall pass away.

"Open, open, open, ye Gates of Dawn"—"Call upon ME and I will answer," and so the Keeper of the Gates of Dawn—of illumination and wisdom, will hear and answer you. You stand alone at the Dawn of *your New Day!* It is glorious! It is Illumination of which we are speaking, not something in books or people—but something in you. "Free gift of Spirit." The time has come for you to stand up in all your glorious Newness and *"Claim your right and press your claim."* Your right to the Tree of Life—this glorious Source of the All.

"Open, open, open, ye Gates of Dawn." Now then, "Son of Man, pass through."

ONE-NESS

"I AM in body just what I am in spirit. I keep my body, mind and soul together. If I say I am going somewhere, I go there in person and make my word good."

"A kingdom divided against itself shall fall"—so has it been with the kingdom of man. He has been divided; his body, his mind and his soul. The three have been battling one against the other, in the darkness of human learning, and hence the kingdom has fallen. What you are in Spirit that you are also in body *in reality*. What you contemplate as the perfect expression, "the picture shown to you on the Mount," is that which you are in reality *in the body*. The mist of human thinking has drawn a veil between you and the perfect out-picturing of your true self. There has been no union, but separation, hence the perpetual crucifixion of the Jesus.

The average man will tell you that his life has been one long struggle, and that he has been eternally in the throes of some problem or other. Can this be the creation of an All-wise Creator? Is it possible that God has created a universe which must and does struggle eternally against a thing called evil, which man is told does not exist?

A caterpillar as such cannot fly. If it were possible to communicate with it, you might talk much about the possibility of its flying, but the caterpillar could not fly and never would fly until it became *self-conscious*—that is until the One-ness of idea and body took hold of it. The moment this union was made, the change necessary to make the flying possible would take place. So is it with the man bound with disease. To tell him he can walk perfectly is to tell him the Truth. He may imagine it, wish it, pray for it, but until the union is made between *mind, soul and body*, nothing will take place. The instant this union is made—the instant One-ness is attained—then the picture shown to him on the Mount, the picture of freedom of body, is made manifest and he jumps with joy, leaping into his new-found freedom.

Do you understand instantaneous healing? The moment you are one with that which you know to be true, that moment the vehicle is made ready to instantly express what *it* knows to be true. Just so we see in the case of the caterpillar, the slow and gradual change in shape and appearance to accommodate the idea with which it has become one. These poor illustrations are but way-markers to the glorious freedom of the sons of the Living God. Little by little we sense the thing, and all the visions you have had begin to move into the plane of the Possible. It is wonderful. Be still.

This perfect union of Jesus and the Christ resurrects the body, and shows it as having flesh and bones and partaking of the foods of every-man, and yet being subject to none of the laws under which he functions. The body that is resurrected from the tomb of human thinking is not again touched by the possibility of the evils of the flesh being made true and manifest. Little by little you are pushing open the door of your new kingdom, and how natural and glorious it all seems as you reach it!

Jesus came to keep soul and body together. He came to save the body. Your soul is already saved.

The thing that had been perishing in the face of abundance is the thing that the Father in you came to save. "I came that ye might have life, and that ye might have it more abundantly" is the language of Scripture. The "I" comes, that the body might have LIFE and that it might have it more abundantly. Do you see what the coming of the Father means to you? Do you begin to *sense* that the "I" in the midst of you is here for the express purpose of saving you from the devastating beliefs of the human mind?

Almost without exception the point of view of the average Truth student is to separate Jesus from the Christ. Jesus crucified fading out of the picture, in the very presence of the All-power which stated through him, 'If you ask anything in my name that give I unto you.' "

No matter how far you have gone in the teaching of duality, no matter what a mess of things you have made, it is all cast away the moment you become one with this glorious true self called the Christ. The veil is rent and you stand before your true self, washed clean from the limitations of your human beliefs. It is glorious. The Christ and Jesus are no more separ-

ated. "That which God hath joined together let no
man (no kind of man with his false teaching) put
asunder."

Do you begin to see the allness of yourself—how
you have within you the possibilities of attainment?
Be still and listen to the deep teachings of the Impersonal Father.

*"It is a blessing to see God in somebody, no matter
who. If you are boastfully seeing God in yourself
and evil in others, then you are only seeing a distorted mental picture. You cannot see God within
yourself unless you see Him within others first. See
God in another and you have seen Him in yourself.
Do you understand? Do you see? If you see him in
another you have seen HIM."*

"No man shall see God and Live"—No man shall
see God, that is, understand and recognize the God-
power, and live any more after the limitations of the
flesh; his whole being shall be changed and made new
and his whole outlook shall be re-born to the new
day. He shall die to the former beliefs and ways of
thinking and existing.

Job's captivity was turned when he saw God in
another. The main issue is that you see God in something or someone—for until you have seen God you
cannot experience the reality of His Presence. Once
you have seen Him He becomes a living reality to
you. An instantaneous help or rather revelator. So we
see and Recognize God in *the Impersonal Father* and
know that we have the possibility of becoming One
with HIM.

Take your attention away from yourself, your problems and your world and fix your vision on the Father, and you will find your universe is being rapidly cleared of the beliefs that were so troublesome. "In a manner that ye know not"—at a time you think not, in a way you know not of—it shall happen. There is nothing to worry about. All is, at this instant, in the safe keeping, of the Father. "Lean on Me—cast your burdens of Me"—do you see, can you do it? If so the problem is solved. The *unafraidness* of the soul that has *seen* God. You are that soul? Do you hear, do you feel the Presence? It is "I." Be not afraid.

The wondrous cleansing fire of Spirit shall not only destroy the great obstacles in your life, but the irritating little things that seem to fray the skeins of peace and harmony. They shall be as nothing. Instead of working out each little problem, the coming of the Presence by the process of Recognition will wipe the slate clean, and cause much to disappear without individual attention. "Heaven and earth are full of Thee." No matter how long you have been in the wilderness of human thinking. No matter how long you have fought against seemingly insurmountable odds—they shall vanish away and the place thereof shall be no more, neither shall the memory of them find acceptance.

"When you allow Christ within you to break down every idol and cast out every foe, when you allow Christ in you to rise and stand there and reign and rule in you, then the Kingdom has truly come and the Will is being done."

The perfect abandon which comes to the soul that takes the Christ way is magnificent. One idol after another goes crashing down. Its going only makes way for the real beauty of the Kingdom to shine through. All the old ideas of personal teaching and following go into the limbo of imagination from which they came, and God is enthroned in the heart and soul of you. The glorious winds of God are blowing free and triumphant through the temple of your being, and the dust of human emotions and beliefs is being swept out.

"Behold I AM HE that should come." Behold! The Presence that is with you at this instant is the Presence which will finally rule absolutely in your life. I am wondering when you are going to relax, get quiet and make the holy union with Me, and be swept into the Kingdom of Heaven which is Here and Now awaiting your coming. Nothing matters in this Presence, for the Government is upon the Shoulders of the I AM, and the fretting and worrying human thought cannot enter. The glorious union of soul and body brings peace and satisfaction; brings instant attainment.

Do you hear? You who read this *very* line. Now is the time for you to experience it. Right *now* at *this* instant. Everything is in perfect order, everything has been cast on the Lord—

Are you afraid of your good? Do you actually believe one-tenth of what you say? Could you accept the good you are asking for? Be very still for a moment. The old idea of working eternally over problems is not the plan of the God-man. That belongs to the being who has separated himself from his soul, and is wandering in the wilderness of human beliefs looking for his "soul-mate," or seeking satisfaction in some outer expression of life. He will walk the face of the whole earth and not find it. Many times may he think he has come within sight of the palace of his dreams, only to find it crumbling away at his approach. The God-man is the one who Recognizes the wholeness of soul and body, and who is willing to accept the good that is due him.

Many persons claim that they are willing to accept the good that is due to them, but few really are. They want their good, but they want to direct just how and when it shall come into expression. It is like a foolish gardener sitting on a fence, in the early spring, imagining that he will direct the oncoming crop of flowers. The lavish abundance which pays no attention to person, place or things, pours out its blessing —infinite, abundant, overflowing, and sends with it the glorious invitation, "Come, eat, drink without price." And he who waits for a personal invitation or a personally conducted tour of the kingdom, *must wait.*

The tree that my enemy planted in his garden turned its lovely head and blossomed in mine. The vines that he planted on his side of the fence crept through the crevice and bore fruit in my garden. So is it with the Universal Love. Nothing can be withheld, and the very thought of personal possession fades into the oblivion of yesterday.

The overflowing abundance of Life goes on. In everything, and through everything. Here, and there, and everywhere. So many blessings you cannot count them. Do you see? Do you hear? Do you *feel* the Presence. You who read this line?

"It is wonderful! It is Love beyond degrees, Mortal mind says it is hypnotism when it sees the glorious freedom of the God-Love. But by the fruits ye shall know, and anything that can change the vile bodies and bring success and prosperity beyond degrees; gifts and talents, life, health, love and everything else, just-ifies itself. The hypnotism of the human mind which continually believes in a series of problems to be solved cannot imagine what would happen if it found itself free from this condition, hence its hatred of the God-Love."

The awakening soul finds it has been hypnotized by the person it called Self, hence we see each man hypnotized to a different state of things. Some are seemingly better than others, but all suffering from the thing called human personality, its birth, family, breeding and rearing. It spends a great deal of time reviewing the history of this personality, relating its shortcomings and its successes, always allying itself to the limitations it finds there. Until this hateful bondage is broken there is nothing to be expected but a series of problems. It is wonderful that we have found a way of escape through "Call no man your Father." If no earthly man is your Father then you cannot partake of the earthly limitations, and hence are not an heir to these troubles and harassing condi-tions. No sooner do you recognize that you are to call no man your father, than you begin to partake of the Heavenly Heritage of the Sons of the Living

God, and the bondage of a human personality falls away. You transcend the beliefs and laws that would have functioned in your life. And you, too, will exclaim in the glorious freedom of the soul, "Thank you, Father." Praise, everlasting praise to Thy Name —it is wonderful! From each of the new-found words will emanate floods of light, and power, which will neutralize the human beliefs of a personality.

THE WORD BECOMES FLESH

"I AM thinking of the things of Spirit that are made flesh, and how the Spirit spiritualizes them. Therefore, Spirit materialized is incorruptible, undefiled and fadeth not away. Hence, being Spirit I AM happy, I am free. Nothing can or does hold me, for I AM Spirit, even though I AM flesh. Yet in my flesh do I see God. My eyes see HIM for MYSELF.

"The word became flesh." "Yet in my flesh shall I see God," etc. We have heard for ages that the Spirit had to be materialized and it is just this new point of revelation that has come to us that causes us to see the practicability of a Spiritual teaching. Always before we have had matter as a thing separate from spirit; a thing upon which spirit acted, but little by little we are seeing the folly of this dual teaching. We are actually moving up into the place where the spirit is becoming materialized, and in our flesh we *are* seeing this oneness. As we come more and more into line with the wonderful teaching of Jesus Christ we understand what was meant when he said "I and My Father are one"—the blending of spirit, the spiritualizing of matter and the materializing of spirit, cause

41

us to become Receiving Stations for the new world of liberation and freedom which heretofore we were unable to receive, because the apparatus was not sufficiently fine to bear the burden of the joy that was contained therein. What could an old dying, broken body possibly do to receive the undying message of Truth? There is nothing in common between the two, and if the Truth could get through, the congested cells of human thinking would not be sufficiently strong to receive the new word. It is wonderful! Can you understand now the walking on water? Now you see the new idea before you. The Word made flesh?

"God is spirit and they that worship him must worship Him in Spirit and in Truth." What will you do with this statement? If God be spirit and must be worshipped in spirit what about the material thinking and the mental striving to worship Him with a fleshly mind that knows something that God does not know? Think it over for yourself, and, if you find that it is so, then cleave to the line and accept your new heritage, and begin to enjoy the fruits of Spirit.

"I AM Alpha and Omega—the first and the last, which is and which was and which is to come, saith the Lord." This interesting piece of information is given us to show that the whole relativity—past, present and future—is swallowed up in the unchanging presence of Spirit. Do you begin to see how Jesus was offering you a full salvation through the Father idea? It is wonderful!

When Jesus was resurrected he had a body of flesh and blood, and yet that body was not subject to any of the laws of the human mind; hence we see that the word made flesh is the state at which we shall arrive when we are ready to take the single standard and accept God as Here and Now—

"*Therefore, Spirit materialized is incorruptible and fadeth not away.*" Do you understand the way to life eternal, and youth eternal? When you identify yourself with materialized spirit you will find that it is incorruptible—that is, it is not to be corrupted by the belief in years, or the ravages of sin and disease. Do you begin to see the futility of all the talk about life eternal, and youth eternal as long as the idea of materialized spirit is not recognized? If you posit first old age that has to be destroyed, then you are defeated before you get started, and a thousand affirmations are not going to break the hateful law of the human mind. But when you awake to the glorious possibilities of the Sons of God, and begin to "*Claim your right and press your claim,*" you will begin to experience the glorious materialization of the Spirit and the Spiritualization of matter, and then you shall know that it is possible.

The glorious freshness of spirit made flesh has nothing to do with the effect that is produced by outside aids, or a straining to make a bold show of an old body with a false appearance of joy. The radiance of spirit gives forth its beauty and freshness of *power* that has nothing to do with anything on the outside.

"Spirit fadeth not away." Where could it fade to since all is spirit? So the last enemy is being swallowed up in victory. The only thing that ever died was a belief, which was engendered by the acceptance of yourself as a human-born thing of human parentage. All things that have a beginning have an end, and in order to escape this rather disastrous thing, it is well for us to begin to see the new way that is offered us. "Yet in my (my own) flesh shall I SEE God." If for one instant you see God in your flesh, you will lose all the beliefs you have had of age and bondage. It is wonderful!

"Nothing Jesus did, or nothing a man can do for you as a person, can save you. You must save yourself."

This is an old idea in new words, in clearer language. "Work out your own salvation," which has been such a bugbear to Truth students, becomes a beautiful opportunity to reveal God in the flesh.

"Jesus did not advocate gifts, He advocated the giver. He did not advocate blessings, He advocated the blesser."

Do you see how your attention is taken from things and placed on the Source of all? Thus you are not to praise the gift but the Giver, and the giver is the God within and without you.

The *blesser* is that to which the praise belongs. The blessing when released, goes its way. "Call not Me (Jesus) good, but one which is in Heaven." Take the attention away from the manifestation and place it on the manifestor, and in this way begin to see the New Day dawn. "Absent from the body—of materialism—and present with the Lord," with the Spirit, which will cause you to come forth with the spiritualized body and universe. It is only with the spiritualized body that the wonders of which we have so long read can be performed. Are you beginning to realize the magnitude of this glorious secret doctrine that is pouring out upon us this day?

"Acquaint now thyself with Him and be at peace, thereby all good shall come unto you." What a wonderful invitation. What will you do with it? You do not need any introduction to God. You do not need any further recommendation, for who has the power to recommend you to God? You do not need any recommendation to speak the word of God, nor any recommendation to acquaint yourself with Him. "Acquaint now thyself with Him (in the midst of you) and be at peace—thereby *all* good shall come unto you."

"Whatsoever God doeth, it shall be forever; nothing can be put to it and nothing can be taken from it."

One of the things that God did was to cause you to come into expression and that, too, in His image and likeness, and this is one of the things to which nothing can be added. Nor from which anything can be taken. The great suffering that you have experienced is due to the fact that you have added many things unto this perfect creation. You have added family, creed, race, birth, human beliefs of all shades and colours, and hence you have gone against the Holy Ghost, as it were, and you are suffering by reason of your own bondage—self-imposed—not from any cruelty of God. "Awake, thou that sleepest and Christ shall give thee light."

Likewise "Nor anything taken from it." So the spiritualized matter will be restored to you, and the gifts and the riches of the joint *heir* shall be revealed, for nothing shall be, or has been taken from you, the perfect manifestation of the Living God. "Then shall the eyes of the blind be opened, and the ears of the deaf unstopped." The glory of God shall be revealed, and so it is. Isn't it wonderful?

"The words that I speak unto you are spirit and are Truth."

That Christ Jesus was without learning is one of the things that caused the wise and prudent to marvel. Watch that you be not led astray by any man's teaching. If the *inner voice* does not *"agree"* with the revelation, then you can set it aside for another day. Follow no man any further than he follows the glorious revelation of Jesus Christ. Watch! "In a moment you think not—I come." Suddenly, as a glorious sun bursting through the clouds, does a new revelation come, and with it the new manifestation. Do you hear—you who read this line?

"It is essential to be led by the Spirit of God, for as many as are led by the Spirit of God, they are the Sons of God. When your Soul goes to heaven then your body must go to heaven also.

"The reason so many lack prosperity and happiness to-day, is that when their souls go to heaven their bodies are left behind. You must keep soul and body together and then you will always be prosperous, healthy and happy. I will not be separated from my Mind, Soul and Body. I keep them all together in heaven, hence I have the key to all understanding, and the key to all underground treasures."

So many people can meditate, and let their minds get into a state of bliss—heaven—and yet have nothing happen on the outside. They experience all the things they desire mentally while the body is going without bare necessities. It is wonderful that this dual manner of life is passing away and man is beginning to take his body to heaven. How is it "Flesh and blood cannot inherit the kingdom of heaven"—and then it is we see the necessity of spiritualizing matter so that it can come through to the plane of Reality? Do you see? The "Flesh and blood" spoken of is the separated idea to which man has lived in bondage to all these long years. It is wonderful! Now comes the wonderful light that mind, soul and body are one, and must be recognized as one, not as three, with three different sets of laws. The three are one—Father, Son, and Holy Ghost—one; wholeness, completeness. Glorious Man, made in the image and likeness of the Father. It is wonderful!

As soon as you recognize the All Presence of God, the *"Spirit of the Consciousness of the Presence of God,"* all this glorious process will begin to make itself manifest to you. Do not look back and crystalize to past conditions. Do not turn into a pillar of salt. Do not go back to the darkness of your former reasoning process. The *voice* has spoken to you direct, out of the depths of your being. He who hears obeys, and will rise and follow the Christ, whithersoever He leadeth.

It is wonderful when you make the unconditional surrendered of yourself and all the human teaching. The unconditional surrender of the government of your life; then you will say with Peter, "I have left all to follow Thee, now what shall I have in return?" Beloved, you shall have in return infinitely more than you ever dreamed of as possible in the old way. The miracles will become natural laws, and you shall go YOUR way. "Who travels alone travels far."

"All mortal habits, systems, ways, ideas, etc., are weights. When you have thrown off the weight and the sin—which does so easily beset you—then you will run the race that is set before you, and wait patiently for Christ to rise in you. Cast all mortal tendencies, personal ideas and fancies out of your consciousness, and consequently out of your system, and you will suddenly experience a feeling of lightness. You will feel like a new creature. It is wonderful to know that when you have made the complete surrender and sacrifice of all these human beliefs and tendencies, that Christ is ready to RISE in you. Just as soon as you make the complete surrender He will rise instantaneously. It is wonderful!"

The complete surrender of all these habits and systems, ways and ideas, etc., is not nearly so difficult as it seems. You are already through with most of them. Most people are already two-thirds of the way into their Divine Heritage. They only need this final acceptance of the Glorious Presence to make it complete, and to see the sudden *Rise* of the Christ within. It is wonderful! Nothing can stay this power, nothing can keep it back.

He WILL rise, and will rise in YOU with healing in His Wings. It is wonderful to have arrived at this state—at the state of full surrender, full relaxation, full consecration, self-denial. 'Here am I, Lord, send me.'

And you have arrived at this state, and are experiencing the new joy of letting the Government be upon the shoulders of this new and wonderful Power, you are beginning to Recognize that the Word has been made flesh, that the flesh is being spiritualized and the spirit materialized. "And His flesh was new and fresh as a babe's."

"The mighty holy love that transcends all limitation goes far into the infinite, the end of which you cannot vision for it is limitless. And it is also without beginning or days, and without end of life; therefore, you can enjoy it and launch out into it, and there will be no end to your life either."

Do you see with what ease this immense gift is placed before you? It is wonderful!

THE FATHER'S WAY

A LION raised in captivity may sense its immense strength, but until he actually becomes conscious of it as an integral part of himself, he might as well be a weakling. Man reasons and theorizes about his God-given ability—but until he actually Recognizes this God-power as the only power within and without, he may experience sickness while *mentally* protesting that "God's perfect child cannot be sick." "You shall find ME when you feel after ME." You shall *feel* after the "ME" within the consciousness. You shall find the Father in the locality that Jesus indicated. "Look not here, nor there, for the Kingdom of Heaven is at hand." The Kingdom of God, the realm of all your unfulfilled dreams and visions, lies within your consciousness. Be still, the Spirit of this glorious message is even at this moment moving upon you; is moving within you; is pressing upon you for recognition.

"You can rid yourself of every negative and untoward condition by your recognition of God within and God without. Recognizing God as walking in

you; talking in you; seeing in you; hearing in you; feeling in you; tasting in you."

Recognition comes not through study of formulae, Recognition comes through that child-like quality of which Jesus said composed the Kingdom of Heaven. Can you accept your good? is the question asked the adult. The answer is either "Yes," or "No," but it is usually something like this, "I would like to accept my good, but do not know how." You do not know how because the more "knowing how" you have in your make-up, the more impossible it is to let the God-self into expression. Think you that you can by begging, by force, or by violence, enter the kingdom? "He that shall hold his tongue shall take a city." He that refrains from trying to *know how,* but will "feel" the Presence will arrive.

"God is actually each one of your five physical senses. God is expressing through the members that are called nose, eyes, mouth, and body. God is your five physical senses. When you realize this, then you will come back to your right state of mind. After this has happened you cannot have bad sight, bad hearing, bad health, or bad anything."

This message is written for *you* alone; you who read this very line. From out the depths of your Being I AM speaking to you—you do not have to mould it into a formula—it already has taken possession of you —suddenly and without struggle the new idea of the PRESENCE within and without and round about you is made manifest. You are Recognizing the ALL-ness of the Inner Consciousness. Every part and parcel of your Universe and body are alive with the Life of Christ, and the drop of water has lost itself in the ocean of Life. It is glorious and wonderful. *"God is your Father. You never had another."*

Suddenly the terrible groaning to be delivered from the body of death—the embodiment of the human beliefs that you have moulded about you by human thinking—gives way before the out-pouring of Light that comes from the Risen Lord. The Jesus stays in the tomb of your own making until the Christ in Him raises Him up. Raises Him up in one-ness. And so is it with you—the Christ within is now awakening by the power of your Recognition of His PRESENCE. Pay no attention to the cold, hard walls of your tomb—take your attention away from appearances and rest them gloriously within on the new Christ. He, it is, who will pick up the body of Jesus and take it from the Tomb of Mortality, and the power that picks *you* up will also provide the way for you. The Christ takes full possession of you.

"Christ is in every joint, every sinew, every bone, every vein, every fibre, every nerve, every cell, every atom, every member of your body."

Do you hear? I am speaking to you from out the tiniest cell of your body—I AM speaking to you—"I AM HERE." Do not put ME aside as a word—just relax into the recognition of the PRESENCE, and then you will see the "height and length and depth and majesty of the Word." "The Word was made flesh." That very Word that was made flesh is awakening and claiming Its temple body. It is glorious! You, who read, deep in your temple body I am calling to

you—I AM speaking to you—I AM singing to you—
every part of the earth is rejoicing. You are experiencing at *this instant* such a flood of healing waters
pouring over you that the sins and beliefs of a thousand lifetimes are being washed out of existence. The
waters are covering the earth. The floods of this
spirit are covering the whole body and are being
absorbed into it. The two are becoming one—the
perfect union of soul and body.

*"The same one is walking in you; is talking in you;
is dwelling in you."*

Do you hear?

"How lovely are thy dwellings, oh Lord of Hosts,"
sings the Psalmist, catching a glimpse of the resurrected man. And we are arriving at that point of expression where we, too, recognize that the dwellings
of the Lord, the Inner Lord, are lovely—altogether
lovely without spot or blemish.

"Be ye therefore perfect, even as your Father in
heaven is perfect."

What a command to be fulfilled. And yet, as you
read, it is being said to you, "Be ye therefore *perfect*,
even as your Father in Heaven is perfect." Yes, said
to *you*, the one who is reading this line. Written for
you, the one who is reading this line. Said to *you*
because it is possible for *you* to accomplish. Said to
you because *now you* understand that the Father in
Heaven is the Inner Lord, the Christ to which Jesus
referred. Once you Recognize the perfection of this
Inner Lord, then the outer must of necessity take on
the loveliness of this Wonderful One. "Be not dismayed, it is I." It is *I*, not another. It is *I*, in the

midst of YOU. The Lord in the midst of you, speaking to *you*. Do you *hear?*

"As many as believed on Him, to them gave He power to become the sons and daughters of God."

TO BELIEVE ON HIM, is to accept Him as real, not as separate but as ONE. The Lord, He is ONE. Do you see the glory of it? You who read? I am speaking to *you* from out the depths of *your* being. I have come at last. At last the veil of human reasoning and teaching has been rent and the glorious vision of your true self is being made manifest to *you* in all its beauty and holiness. As you read the Voice is speaking within the depths of *your* being. A new word is given *you*. A new unwritten, unspoken word is being conveyed to *you*, which is the open sesame to the King's Treasures.

How very wonderful that this very book was written with no other mission in life than to bring this message to *you*. This very book was written for *you* alone, for *you* the All-one. This time *you* cannot escape *Me*. I have come. Behold, they shall not all sleep.

There is only one way to have perfect peace. "He shall keep him (the body) in perfect peace whose mind is stayed on Him." What a glorious revelation and how easy it is to keep the mind stayed on Him— when you know who the "Him" is and what it represents, and how everything that you Recognize as true of Him is true into expression. Hence, just now, you either accepted that it was *easy* to keep the mind stayed on Him, or else *you* injected your human thought and said it is difficult. Presently there will be no going back to the cherished human conditions you accepted. No matter how long you have accepted them. No matter if ten thousand people have experienced them and found them true. It is no longer true for you because you have stepped up into the new realm of the PRESENCE.

Do *you* hear ME say *you* HAVE stepped up into the new realm of Reality? Do *you* hear? Do *you* have to discuss that with another? Not if you hear. Because if *you* hear it is too precious to discuss with another. The one who has likewise accepted the New State of Consciousness will recognize *you* on Life's Highway and give *you* the sign. Things that are true are so obvious they do not need to be discussed. Christ tells you either personally or impersonally all that is necessary.

"When the Spirit of Truth has come it shall guide you into all Truth." When the recognition of your Inner Lord, the Christ Consciousness, takes place, that Recognition shall guide you into all Truth. Not a part of it, but into ALL TRUTH. All that you have been seeking, lo, these many years. It is wonderful!

"I will walk in you and talk in you."

"I AM so glad that God in one man is a majority."

"Are you that ONE Man? You can be, in fact, you are when you Recognize the "Presence of the Spirit of the Consciousness of God in the midst of you." It is wonderful!

"Is this HE that should come, or look we for another?" When you stop looking for *another* you will find the One. And when you have found the One, you will cease the wandering to and fro in the realm of human knowledge. And all this is the free gift of the Father within.

"Thank you, Father," was the full word of Recognition used by Jesus in bringing forth the manifestation necessary, whether it was a piece of gold, or a loaf of bread; a restored, whole arm, or a perfect eyesight. The same simple Recognition preceded everything, and to-day we are beginning to Recognize the same privilege, and to be bold enough to say "Thank you, Father," for the unmanifest good which we have accepted. No sooner has this been said from the centre of your being than the realization takes place, and the "Manna from heaven"—the unseen substance —falls to earth and materializes into whatever form is necessary that instant.

Go not out to clamour with the midnight and the storm of human reasoning. No man ever caused a seed to grow by opening it. No seed kept perpetually under the microscope of human thought ever germinated. Gathering human testimony as to how the law works does not make it work. The child will set it into motion by accepting and Recognizing it as possible and present. It is wonderful! Be still. All the old ruts in human consciousness that you have been worshipping have to be filled full of the new substance of Mind and made level and smooth. Be still.

IF ANY LACK WISDOM

"If any of you lack wisdom let him ask of God, who giveth to all liberally and upbraideth not; and it shall be given him. But let him ask in faith, nothing doubting, for he that doubteth is like the surge of the sea driven by the wind and tossed. For let not that man think that he shall receive anything of the Lord." James i. 5-7.

Aren't you glad that the day of seeking your information from a man-teacher is over? Aren't you glad that the word has come to you which will free you from all the new and old systems of Truth, and give you the pure gold of wisdom? Aren't you glad that you have discovered you have at last begun to return to the things that you left to follow after personalities and systems of Truth? It is wonderful!

Such a flood of joy comes with the reading of this holy offer, "If any lack wisdom." If you lack wisdom "ask of God." Aren't you glad you do not have to ask a teacher, or a preacher, or the starter of some new and original system of Truth? "If any lack wisdom." It does not make any difference who that "any" is.

We do not have to have any more intercessors. We

can come direct to the Source of all Wisdom. We do not have to "ask some person"—it says, "let him ask of God." The wonderful revelation of each word of this glorious offer thrills you as you think of the many things you have wanted to know, and the many and various answers you have had from people. This offer is for you. You, the reader of this line. Is there anything you want to know?

As you read on you see "who giveth to all liberally and upbraideth not." Do you catch the significance of the word "liberally." You do not need to be afraid that the wisdom you receive from God will not fit the issue—for He will give it to you liberally and will not upbraid you for your spiritual lean-ness. He will not stand before you as a great wisehead, looking down on you as a poor wretch who knows nothing. He will not pose before you as one of those sanctified souls who is toiling for God, and who holds the secrets of Life, and wonders if he dare pass a little of this information on to you. He is the one who "Giveth liberally and upbraideth not." Do you hear? Aren't you glad? Do you not begin to see the joy of travelling alone? How it is that the wondrous revelation is being made to you? Aren't you glad? "And it shall be given him." Not a shadow of doubt. Direct, right from the shoulder without any reservations. "And it shall be given him." Do you hear—"it shall be given you." Was there ever a clearer and cleaner proposition made to you—and direct between you and God, and no intermediary, or no learned soul that first smirches the precious word and strains it through his befogged mentality. "And it shall be given unto him." Not only wisdom, but "Ask what ye will" is another statement for you to contemplate. I said "What you will." Not what someone else thinks is best for you, not what you suppose is enough for you—"What you will, and it shall be given unto you."

Be still and contemplate where the beautiful revelation is leading you. You are kicking free from the letter of somebody's teaching, and coming into the inner sanctuary of your soul and finding there yourself and God. Yourself as much a partaker of this glorious Truth as anybody. Isn't it wonderful? Aren't you glad? And that is not all. "Ask and ye shall receive," "knock and it shall be opened," "seek and ye shall find." The measure is full, pressed down, shaken together and running over. The glorious storehouse of God is bursting the human limitations you have put upon it.

On and on the revelation goes to the point of "Before you ask I will answer, and while you are yet speaking I will give it unto you," and at last you are glimpsing the Absolute which shows you the omnipresence of everything here and NOW.

But there must be some catch in all this glorious thing, the human mind says. I have asked time and time again, and I have known whole rooms full of people to ask and nothing happen. If you think there is some catch to it, or if you think it is not true, absolutely, then why do you not throw the whole thing overboard and be done with it? You cannot, because the soul of you knows that it is the absolute Truth, and that the moment you "click" as it were, with this wonderful revelation, you will see the revelation, the manifestation, the glory of the Risen Lord. It is wonderful!

"But, let him ask in faith, nothing (not anything—do you hear?) doubting." Isn't the amplitude of the "Nothing doubting" amazing. It thrills you even if you are only half believing it. Such a sweeping statement could only be made of an Infinite Power, could only be made by an omnipotent, omniscient Being. You are being ushered into the inner of Inners. "Let him ask in faith, nothing doubting." So wonderful. Can you see the Absolute faith in the power. No matter what someone has said or proven—you and this glorious thing, Absolute Faith, which is nothing more or less than the Recognition of the fact that there is such a thing as an omnipresent God. Here and NOW. Do you hear, the Spirit of this glorious thing is coming into being right now as you read. Absolute Faith —radical Faith—all the kinds of stay-put faiths you can imagine which will be melted down into the simple and child-like acceptance that GOD IS.

You have tried everything else and failed—why not try this absolute, radical Faith—this Recognition of God as being here and now and everywhere, and as being amply able to run the universe without any help from, but with the perfect co-operation of you. What universe? Your universe. You are the co-operator of this glorious Power.

"Nothing doubting" is enough about which to write a book. "Nothing—not anything—not a single thing—doubting." No, not even the tiny thing that you think is too small to bother with, nor the great big thing that you think is too large, or the hopeless thing that you know now cannot be rectified. Not anything doubting. Nothing doubting. Not a single thing. Do you hear? Do you see? Do you feel? It is so wonderful, for the Recognition of this power is freeing the re-constructing element of life, the transforming power which is to make you anew, or rather, which is to reveal the wonderful You.

And to think that this wonderful offer should be made to you. The poor little downtrodden you, or the terrible puffed-up, egotistical creature who is so tired and sick of yourself. Why it is wonderful! and of course you are glad, for this glorious revelation is going to buoy you up on new pinions, and destroy all the ugly personal thing which has thought itself so much. It is going to release you, and make you clean and honest. So aren't you glad that you have found it, and aren't you glad that you are ready to accept God as the only source of Wisdom? The wisdom that you now receive is going to free you from the hateful bondage you have been under so long.

"For he that doubteth is like the surge of the sea, driven by the wind and tossed. Let not that man think that he shall receive anything of the Lord." Like the surge of the sea, driven by the wind and tossed, is almost like a character sketch of most Truth people.

How many times have you been driven by the wind and tossed about from one teaching to another? Crying within your soul, "Oh if I could find Him." Do you see, beloved, the power that indecision has over you—when there is no Recognition of the Presence—the great and terrible shifting and changing of indecision sets in and makes life one long confusion? Isn't it wonderful that we are beginning to get at the very basis and root of what seemed to be the trouble? "For without Faith it is impossible to please Him."

This is putting into poetry a very homely everyday law of life. Without recognizing that a thing exists you will never be able to use it. Sounds almost stupid, but that is all there is to it. Without recognition of the God-power you cannot manifest any of the God qualities, and so you stand on the outside of the temple. Until this radical faith, or recognition, comes or is put into use, you cannot have revealed to you the glorious manifestations that are all about you.

Radical, absolute faith. The blandest kind of acceptance; without reservation, without the introduction of human doctrines or opinions.

"I have never seen the righteous forsaken or his seed begging bread." Do you hear? Are you afraid to step out on the promises and accept your good? Are you afraid of this radical reliance? Are you afraid to believe absolutely and finally in the presence of God?

The Name of the I AM that you are serving transcends all conditions and limitations. Do you hear? I speak to you. We are beginning to sense the Presence —the new planes of expression are beginning to appear. The things that you desire when asked for in this place of Recognition will come into manifestation. Be still and know.

Once you recognize this Presence—nothing doubting—you will then know the freedom of the Sons of the Living God:

"The Spirit of the Consciousness of the Presence of God is the Source of all Supply, and will Satisfy Every Good Desire."

Little by little the Inner Voice is bringing to your attention the truth that is hidden in this masterly revelation. New vistas and avenues are coming into view. Old ways and methods, are being consumed by the larger view of life, controlled by the harmonious Presence of God. Those things which are necessary for the *Son of God* to have are already in place.

"The night is far spent and the day is at hand. Let us, therefore, cast off the works of darkness, and let us put on the garments of Light." The night of human belief and personal teaching is far spent, and THE DAY revelation is again here and NOW. So many discrepancies in the night of human thinking that never would come right, and suddenly we realize the power of this human thinking is far spent—it is running down—it is only spending the energy it gained by being believed in as true.

Comes now the invitation, "Let us cast off the works of darkness and let us put on the garments of Light." Was ever an invitation more welcome, and was ever an invitation more possible to you than now? Now that you have your glorious radical Faith, your glorious Recognition of the Presence of the Father here, there and everywhere.

The old darkness of human thinking with its endless making evil, and trying to get rid of it, must give place to the Light which is even now enveloping us, and making us ready for the New Day. Do you hear? Can you say "Thank you, Father," and mean it now?

"I will pour out my spirit upon you, I will make known my words unto you. When you are ready I will do the works." Isn't is glorious? The Master is here, and now making the way clear and plain for you.

"Verily, verily, I say unto you, the hour is coming

and NOW IS, when the dead shall hear the voice of the Son of God and they that hear shall live." You are beginning to realize how it is that the night is far spent and that the day is at hand. The new and glorious idea of Life is being made manifest to you.

"If any of you lack wisdom, let him ask of God who giveth to all liberally and upbraideth not; and it shall be given him. But let him ask in Faith, nothing doubting, for he that doubteth is like the surge of the sea, driven by the wind and tossed. For let not that man think that he shall receive anything of the Lord."

THE SHADOW OF SPIRIT

"As LONG *as you stand in the light of truth you are bound to have a shadow. This shadow, which is cast in the material world, is the out-pouring of all desirable things; plenty to eat—plenty to drink—plenty to year—money, substance, expression—manifestation in whatever form needed.*"

The ease with which a shadow is cast is the ease with which manifestations must come into the pictures when the Recognition of the Presence is made. Nothing is actually done, as far as a shadow itself is concerned, to make it appear. You step in the light and the shadow automatically *is*. You step into the Light of understanding! That is, you Recognize the Presence, and the manifestation must come into being, without effort and without great acclaim. It is silent and natural, it appears the moment you step into the light. Are you going to accept this *New* Day and the *New* Way of manifestation, or are you going to try to *make* the shadows appear? You see how hopeless it is to make shadows appear unless the Light is there. It cannot be done, no matter however hard you try. And in reality you have to *let* a shadow appear—you cannot do anything with it. You cannot make it go away—it is a thing that *is*, and it appears naturally. It is a reproduction, after a fashion, of you, and so all manifestation that you see in your universe is a reproduction of some state of your consciousness.

"Signs follow." Shadows follow the stepping into the Light. The moment—at the identical instant—you come into the Light the shadow *is*. At the moment you ask, even before you have time to formulate the petition, *it is*. Do you begin to see something that is quicker than the so-called thought process? "Closer is HE—the I AM—than breathing, nearer than hands and feet." Pretty close, isn't it? And when you think that within this I AM is all the power, then it begins to look interesting, and begins to look as though all that is necessary is the *Recognition* on our part of the *Presence*.

In a Belgium fish market a husky fish-wife cleaned her fish for years on a painted board, which she threw into the fish cart at night. One day an art connoisseur happened along and noticed it. He bought it for a few sous, and discovered that it was a valuable old masterpiece. Suddenly it became a thing of great price—it was there all the time—but as long as it was unrecognized it remained without value. Do you see? The *Recognition* having been made, any fish-wife that had dared to pass a knife over the surface of the same board would have been arrested as a vandal. Do you see? Why not get quiet and let this glorious nearness of the Presence come into manifestation?

Thousands of illustrations have been given from time to time, but all these are thrown aside and man finds his own *Presence* by a way that no other man knows.

"Send me—send Me," says the voice of the awakened Soul. Send me into the new-expression of the Son of the Living God. It is wonderful! and So It Is.

The new teaching—or the new Revelation—is the oldest thing in the world. It is so simple we stumble over it. It is the *acceptance* of the Presence as Here and NOW, and in any form that is necessary, to set absolute harmony into manifestation.

You will always have a shadow as long as you walk in the light, and no matter how many shadows are cast, nothing is taken from you and nothing is added to you. Do you see that "Nothing is added to the Word (you) of God and nothing can be taken from it"—all else is but the shadow that is cast forth to offset some human belief in a power opposed to God?

"The Lord is My light"—then I will always have a manifestation—a shadow. Do you begin to see the Revelation that is made by this illustration? That all the manifestations of the human world are but shadows—that we have given them power and have gone through the Adam process of naming everything, and endowing things with evil power to harm or hurt us? It is not impossible for a man to be frightened at his own shadow. This silly thing has happened—and this idea can be carried on to a place where he knows that he has been frightened by mental shadows of things that never did exist even in the material world.

Do you begin to catch a glimpse of the Light? Are you beginning to see also the shadow that is being cast? "Arise, shine for thy light has come and the glory of God has risen upon you." Your business is to arise to the point of *Recognition* and the rest will take care of itself.

"I AM the Light of the world"—the *I am* in you *is* the Light of your universe. "A city that is set upon a hill (a state of consciousness which recognizes the Presence) cannot be hid."

Remember that the Light of God came before the human symbols of light. You have but to read through the beginning of Genesis to see that the light was commanded to shine before the sun, the material symbol of light, was brought out. We are speaking of Light, that is, of a higher rate of vibration than any light that could be made by material means. It is the Light that could penetrate the thickest wall, or the deepest depths.

"God hath made me to laugh, so that all that hear will laugh with me." The glorious laughter of joy that must thrill through your being once you have *Recognized* the Presence—"God hath made me to laugh, so that all that hear will laugh with me." And this was addressed to Sarah, who symbolizes that state of consciousness which says: "I am too old to have a new idea or to grasp the new way." "I have made too many mistakes," etc., etc. This glorious thing happened to her—to show that no matter what state you are in, the new idea will be born—to carry out the words of the Scriptures. "Anything is possible to God." You who read—no matter how old, how young, or how worn-out you may be with systems, words and beliefs—you too shall say, "God hath made me to laugh, so that all that hear will laugh with me." You know what kind of laughter that is—it is not a stage laugh, a make-believe laugh—it is one of those glorious ringing laughs that is the natural expression of a joy which cannot be restrained. It is this real quality that makes it contagious—so that all the others of your universe laugh with you.

"If you are subject to the Spirit of Light, then you are instantly released from the evils of the shadow world—of the material world. By not understanding these shadows you have endowed them with power over you. Walk in the Light."

The Wisdom of God brings understanding from within out. The wisdom of the human mind is from the outside in. The human mind judges from appearances, and hence its deductions are always erroneous. It accepts the mirage as real, simply because it appears to be real.

"This table (referring to a banquet table laden with choice viands) is but the outer expression or shadow of the condition of the consciousness within. It is the out-picturing which shows what I (the I AM) have in the store-house for you."

Do you begin to sense the New order that is being established? No more are we trying to demonstrate the "table," we are going back of all this to the point of *Recognition* which causes the table to appear where the table and banquet are necessary. "Thou preparest a table before me in the presence of mine enemies—my cup runneth over." As soon as you step into the Light the shadow is produced, and that, too, in the presence of your enemies. In the presence of the greatest of all enemies—the belief in a power opposed to God—all the enemies of belief may be present; but they will be as naught in the presence of the new shadow that is cast by your coming into the Light. No matter if your universe is filled with beliefs that substance is impossible to you, just the moment you *Recognize* the *Presence* the shadow is cast into expression, and the *"Spirit of the Consciousness of the Presence of God is the source of all supply—fills all space; no space is vacant thereof—and meets every good desire."*

"You are not mourning any more because you have found IT. You are rejoicing because it is materially manifested in your life. Therefore, you can rejoice that you are meek enough to let your Saviour come into your life—the very material life."

Do you hear? It distinctly says, *"You are not mourning any more."* Do you hear? It is so. And do you hear the words, *"Because it is materially manifested"?* The day has come when we are to see the thing as a reality. The day is here when we are to handle "IT" with our hands, and touch IT—that is, the day of beautiful phrases and highflown theories about God and the Universe is over, and the day of Reality and Manifestation is at hand. The importunity of the Prodigal, knocking at the gate of his castle, has sprung open wide the door of the materialized manifestation.

It is no good to talk longer about God being all Good and the All supplier, etc., the time has come when these words must be made manifest in a way there is no mistaking. There must be no more of the old theorizing—the promises are ready to come into manifestation in such a way that the man in the street can see, hear, and be instructed in the Reality of God. Do you believe, Beloved? It is so.

"The first heaven and the first earth are passed away"—the first heaven and the first earth represent the exalted and theoretical idea we gained by the study of words. We were always imagining all sorts of things that should be true and *were* true theoretically, but which manifests only in a very limited degree on the earth. We finally have come to a place where we are finished with theory, we are tired of words and promises, we are ready to have the "New heaven and the New earth" of which we read—the actual manifestation of something tangible and real. We do not want to live any longer in the imaginary world which says "all is good," but which manifests nothing but evil on the plane of the physical. *We are claiming our right and pressing our claim* to that which we have been told is ours as the Sons of the Living God. We are laying claim to the manifestation of the perfect body, which is the resurrected body of which Jesus spoke, and which he showed to his disciples as having flesh and blood and which lived in the world but not of it— which had new and wonderful powers as natural laws working in its members. This is our heritage. *"Claim your right and press your claim."*

"The New Heaven and the New Earth," is that Spiritualized matter, and materialized Spirit which makes all one and one all. Man, then, is one with the whole universe and it rushes to obey him.

"Now, how can anything be withheld from man when the doors of the universe are flung open to him? For the Angel of the Lord has descended into

the centre of all, and the Oneness of Life in mineral, vegetable, animal and human kingdoms is established." "All things work together for the good." *Everything is working with you in this new heaven and new earth. The very thing you are seeking is seeking you. "Here I AM, Lord, send me, send me."*

"Here I am, Lord, send me, send me," out into expression. The glorious freedom and willingness to be sent out into expression in the New Day that is even now dawning, bespeaks the truth that you have left the shadows of human belief of former limitations in the valley, and have not turned back. Now you are ready to *let* go of them—to let the dead beliefs bury their dead. You are in a New Day.

"There is no limitation, there is no terror, there is no lack. There is no want. The Abundance of the Fullness of the Consciousness of Good, no space is vacant of the fullness thereof, has made this so to you. Realize this so vividly in your material universe, in your material body, that you see it." "Yet in my flesh shall I see God." *"You are the begetter, the conceiver, and the Father-mother of whatsoever you "vision-ize." You are the bringer-out of the Vision which is shown to you on the Mount."*

You see that to vision a thing is to merely put it into reality. You are merely aligning yourself with this glorious power that is here, there, and everywhere.

"Human intelligence has gravity, the same as the earth has gravity, and it tends to go so far up and then descends, but the Divine Mind transcends all gravita-

tion. It transcends all belief, and all expressions of limited degrees, mentally and Spiritually. It is that which will lift you above the realm of the beliefs which cause you to gravitate earthward, and causes you to ascend to the plane of perfection."

The human intelligence which judges from appearance has the weight of human belief which holds it down. As soon as the human mind ceases to believe in a thing, then the weight of that thing goes. A fruit that has been accepted as poisonous, on being discovered free from poison, is instantly released from the gravity of the belief in poison, and so on. When you see that the gravitation of the earth belief of lack has no more power over you, you will ascend above a place of dollars and cents into a place of *Infinite Substance*. Do you begin to see? You who read this line.

"If thou knewest the gift of God." You are beginning to know this "*gift*" from God—this precious gift of Revelation that is even at this instant being made manifest to you. "If thou knewest the gift of God" you would not want any more for anything. This gift is so complete and full and so far above the divided idea.

"The gift of God is eternal Life"—what are you going to do with it? Is it just another statement? Are you going to accept your gift? "Stir up the gift that is in thee." It is already there, stir it up into expression by *Recognizing* that it is there.

THE MAGNET OF LIFE

THIS *is eternal life to know the true and living God.*
"I AM the magnet of salvation and will draw all men unto ME. If you are truthful in that which is least, then you can be truthful in that which is great. You can arouse God in your consciousness as God was aroused in the ship at Galilee. It is good to have this faith which is realization."

The Faith which is Realization and Recognition of the Presence is that which suddenly becomes aware of the fact that, no matter how far astray your boat has gone, and into what depths it has drifted, there is a Christ within which, when Awakened or Recognized, will instantly restore harmony, and make the human waves of fear and belief subside, and perfect peace ensue. Do you begin to see the glorious instantaneous effect of this Recognized Presence?

"I AM the magnet of salvation and will draw all men unto ME," is the essence of encouragement, for we begin to see and understand the law which says, "Ye did not choose me, but I chose you." The power has chosen you as one of the vessels into which the glorious overflowing expression of Life is to be

poured. And Now You are beginning to realize your mission in life as a bearer of the Word, the living, vibrating, substance of God.

"He made himself as God" was one of the things with which they charged Jesus, and yet what else could he make Himself as? He was God-created, and God-sustained in a God-Universe. You, too, will come to that place where you will make yourself as God, because you will Recognize absolutely no other than the One God, Lord of Lords and Master of the whole Creation, and you will accept the inspired word that you were made in His image and likeness. And what could be more glorious than this blending with the Universal God and the doing away with all the little man-gods that roam about?

"Perfect love casteth out fear." "*For your sakes I—THE I AM—am revealing to you that there is no fear, except that engendered by your human belief. There is nothing to fear in My Kingdom. My stand is independent of every mortal. I have come treading the wine-press alone. I detach Myself from everything.*"

"*All people are the children of God.*"

"*God is wiping away all tears from your eyes. I AM taking away your sorrows. God looks out of your beautiful eyes. He sees that it is very good.*"

"*So many blessings you cannot count them. Christ in you and Christ in ME will make the whole world what it ought to be.*"

Do you hear, you who read these lines? God wipes out the belief in a personality, and gives you the glorious materialized spirit. For the moment you Recognize this glorious Revelation, *"I AM here, I AM there, I AM everywhere,"* in truth and in deed, you will see it into manifestation. "Prove me now and see if I will not open windows in heaven and pour out a blessing ye cannot receive"; it will be so much more than the human mind has ever dreamed possible; it will be along lines that the human mind has been unable to accept as being possible. It will be so everlastingly complete and full that you will never doubt again. You will be like the man who found the pearl of great price and sold all to posses it—and when he had it, he buried it in a field—in a new state of consciousness. Now do you see how it is that "I have come to tread the wine-press alone"—how it is that you have to receive your own wine (inspiration)? Just imagine it, you are at the point of something wonderful. "You are treading the wine-press alone." You are the source of your own inspiration. Jesus came, stating in a way and manner which we can hear and appreciate, and at the same time stripping the glorious word of all human bondage or personality.

"Look out of your beautiful eyes." Are you beginning to note the direct message? You are told to do things only that you are capable of doing. *Look out of your beautiful eyes*—go ahead—look! Yes, it is something like the feel of "Stretch forth your hand"—there is something there that does not appear on the surface. "Be whole" contains something so big and so wonderful that, if you pause for a moment, you have to exclaim:"I want to, but I do not see how," and you do not, and you will not until you come again to the point where you will rise to the issue and accept, blindly, as far as the human sense is concerned—blindly,

as far as the human reasoning and appearances are concerned—with the fearlessness and audacity of a child taking its own and using its own. It is wonderful! Do you begin to see a little what the NEW Day is revealing to us?

Fret not yourself—be not anxious—just be still and hear the fluttering of the unmanifest bird of freedom, trying its wings for the new flight.

"There is nothing to fear in my Kingdom"—My Kingdom is Here and Now, and you are in it the moment you Recognize the Father as Omnipresent and Eternal.

There is nothing to fear in my Kingdom and the kingdom is everywhere. Do you hear, you who read this line? Be still. "There is nothing to fear in My Kingdom."

Jesus did not give absent treatments for he knew I AM everywhere always.

Perhaps that is one of the most revolutionary statements ever made in the field of Metaphysics. Thousands of people say they give absent treatments, and they speak a truth, for when you give an *"absent"* treatment it is you, the person, that is giving it; but when the I AM speaks the word it is not *absent*, it is there. And do you see the way in which you, as the avenue through which this glorious power is coming into expression, are being used?

"I AM here, I AM there, I AM everywhere"—is what we have all been saying about God, and so it is with you or your patient. "If you make your bed in hell, I AM there just the same; and if you go to the

uttermost parts of the earth, I AM there." At last we are beginning to glimpse some of the wonders.

"So many blessings, you cannot count them. Beyond your highest affirmation lie the fields of endless joy, beyond degree. The Abundance of the Fullness of the Attributes of God is NOW manifest in your body and soul. The manifest Christ reveals what the unmanifest Christ conceals."

"The manifest Christ reveals what the unmanifest Christ conceals." That which *is* and *has been* eternally true will manifest itself to you, just as soon as the union is made between the soul and body, and a fit dwelling place is made for the manifestation of spirit.

"Beyond your highest affirmation lies the fields of endless joy, beyond degree." Beyond everything you can think or ask—is the way it is written in the Scriptures, and the things that are not seen and heard, and have not entered into the heart of man are the things that are beyond your highest affirmation. Beyond the human idea of good lies the reality of God, which is above all of the pairs of opposites.

"The abundance of the fullness of the attributes of God is NOW manifest in your body and soul."

What are the attributes of this God of whom you have thought so much, but the freedom into expression of the idea that has been pressing upon you for out-picturing all these years. The attributes of God, the Abundance of the Attributes of God. "If I attempt to count them, they are as the sands of the seas —do you see? This very abundance is pressing upon you Now—right Now on you, as you read, and as I write, what do you say? Why, I believe you are making an agreement with me, just as we are both making agreement with God in all that He says.

"If fear assails you, do the things you fear. There is no need to pray; only praise God day and night in all things."

There is no need to pray, sounds sacrilegious after you have been told to "pray without ceasing"—but the true prayer is merely the praise and constant Recognition. Do you begin to see the difference between the letter and the spirit? We Praise God always by Recognizing His Presence in everybody and thing. The old idea of prayer was to tell God that he was a great and terrible God, and that you were the worm of the dust, in need of something that you did not think you ought to have, but at the same time you wished you could have. "Without faith it is impossible to please Him."

"Blessings are like things bought on the instalment plan, if you do not pay for them, they will be taken away. If you do not praise God for them, they will disappear."

Return to God-consciousness, the mind that Jesus had. Contact this Mind and you will be free; the Spirit within you will return. Whatsoever you desire will come to pass.

The Glory of God Here and Now lifts you far beyond all lack, fear and limitations."

Beloved, do you not see that the Glory of God's Love is at this moment reaching you with its great awakening power, and that you are beginning to experience the feel of the Presence? Can you, in face of all the beliefs, accept the Glory of God as Here and Now, and deliberately place yourself in the position of receiving the gifts of Spirit? To be lifted by the glory of God here and now, the flesh must be spiritualized by the Recognition of your oneness. Jesus the Christ—Jesus-Christ, oneness—wholeness, completeness. You, as the spiritualized manifestation of God, are ready to be lifted to a place where the former things and laws and beliefs do not, cannot touch you, no matter what the human law says. "If I be lifted up." If you are ready to accept the good of God here and now, you are also prepared to make your temple ready to receive the glorious new vibration of the Now, and experience the feeling of being lifted beyond all lack, fear and limitation, and away from all adverse conditions, no matter from what source they issue. Come apart from among them and be quiet, be still, and know.

"Only when you put a seal upon your lips and go within to the Me of you, and identify yourself with this, can you taste of the glories of the Kingdom. You will not talk about healings, but you will be in a place where there is nothing to heal. You will be silent, serene, joyous."

The seal placed upon your lips is not the seal that many think. It is a cessation from argument about the truth, and this gives opportunity for speaking the Truth. There is such a difference in talking the Truth and talking about the Truth. The latter will get you nowhere, except into arguments from which you will be unable to extricate yourself. What do you care about others' opinions, beliefs and knowledge? They are all subject to change without notice. Last week's newspaper is not interesting to you to-day; the news is dead, and so is it with the opinions and beliefs of others; before you know it they are worth nothing and are cast aside.

Unadulterated Faith is the faith of a child because adult faith would be sure to be adulterated with human opinions and limitations. No wonder the kingdom of heaven is made up of children. The "Unmingled Love" is the God-love which is not moved by the human emotions to do something special for one and not for another. The unmingled love is that which frees from fear and limitations—it is the pure God-Love passing from God to man.

"Take all you want, but don't forget the best." How do you like that invitation? Dare you to accept it—could you take the best? Would that be right? What do you think—would a child take the best piece of candy if offered the choice? Would you, if you were alone? Well, I am just asking you a few questions—you answer them for yourself—"but be sure you take the best." Do not forget—do you hear?

You can speak the word of God with fluency and with a lovely inspiration, if you will let God speak in you. "Ye need only open your mouth, and the words will be supplied." But if you are not absent from the body at the same time, you will not know what to do with the body, and finally you will end by making no speech. That is all there is to successful lecturing— when you are ready God will use you, and speak the Word through you, and make you a glorious channel of the inspiration of Spirit. The same power has a thousand attributes to express through you.

"*When you have cancelled all your preconceived ideas and opinions about yourself as a personality, then you shall live forever. We are His, whether expressed or unexpressed. I will set you free from every undesirable thing.*"

"And this is Life eternal to know ME"—you cannot know ME as long as you insist that you are a thing apart from me—born in sin and conceived in iniquity, and full of all uncleanness and evil. You cannot know Me as long as you identify yourself with a human destiny, and feel that you must fulfill that destiny. You cannot know ME as long as you think there is another power apart from Me which is said to be less powerful, but which appears to be more so. Awake! thou that sleepest—the New Day, the New Idea—that which transcends the human beliefs has come.

"*I will set you free from every undesirable thing*"— either you believe it or you do not. If you do not, it does not matter how much you talk and argue about it, it will not change anything—if you do, it will be fulfilled. I do not know how—I cannot imagine—I have no way of knowing, so why should I bother to find out? God has a way—"His ways are past finding out" —so why worry any more how it is going to take place? I said, "*I will set you free from every undesirable thing*," and I mean it. Whether you can accept it or not, it is true.

"For we know that the whole creation groaneth and travaileth in pain together until NOW."

And not only they, but ourselves also, which have the first fruits of Spirit, even we ourselves groan within ourselves, waiting for the adoption—to wit, the redemption—of our body.

We see, then, that this wonderful word of freedom has not come at the wrong time—for "the whole creation groaneth and travaileth in pain together" until NOW—until Now, until you Recognize the Presence of God, your whole universe has been groaning and travailing in pain, and likewise you have been awaiting the adoption—to wit, the redemption—of your body. The body that has been lost in material beliefs, of sin, sickness and fear, is to be redeemed by the union of the spirit and matter. The prodigal is to return to his Father state of consciousness, and receive the robe and the ring and the fatted calf. The body is to be freed from the laws of human thinking, and is to take on that spiritualized flesh of which Jesus spoke, and which he showed to his disciples.

"By closing your conscious mentality and stilling it, the Inner man will speak and will unfold. By closing all material books the Book of Life will open to you, and reveal its hidden secrets. The Book of Life and Heaven in the Heavenly state of consciousness is opened in you. In that book you find your new name written—the name which no man shall pronounce, and the great revelations of Truth come forth and loosen the seven seals."

Think of the Book of Life being opened before you—do you begin to see? You who read this line—that looking past all material books you shall read the true message in *"The"* Book, and find your new name written therein.

"When man becomes God-conscious, then he knows himself to be the Fatherhood degree of Spirit or Truth. Knows himself to be the Motherhood degree of Spirit; knows himself to be the Sonship degree of Spirit or body. The Jesus-Christ man, or the perfect expression of His True self."

All our troubles have arisen from the fact that man has striven to make over his consciousness and body— he has worked with them, trying to make them come up to the standard of the vision shown to him at the moments of his highest realization. Now he is learning that the soul and body must be one in the Invisible, as well as in the visible.

SUPPLY

"THERE *is no lack in the great Universal Mind Sub-stance, in which you live, move, and breathe, and have your being. The same flow of substance which fed the five thousand with the two fish and five loaves, could have fed the whole world at the same time, had it been necessary. There is no limitation, and you are the manifestor of that substance. It is wonderful. You are the expressor of the same, to be brought forth into manifestation in these last times.*

It is wonderful that you can tune in on this Great Universal Mind Substance by relaxing your conscious mentality, your limited human intellect, and being still, so that the Christ within can act, live, move, and have His being in you, to will and to do in you His own good pleasures, for in you He lives and moves and has His being, at the same time you live and move and have your being in Him."

By relaxing the conscious mentality—by letting go of the thing that continually tries to demonstrate sub-stance, we come into tune with the very Substance itself. No sooner have you accepted the idea as the Child of the Living God, and made your agreement therewith, than you cease the endless trying to get something out of the Father, and you come home to the fatted calf, the robe, and the ring which await you, no matter how prodigal you have been. As soon as you relax the conscious mentality, you make way for the in-rush of the God substance—it comes into visibility freely and of its own accord. The lost is found. For "In Him you live and move and have your being," and also in you He lives and moves and has His being. Now then, prepare to let Him into expression in your everyday life, by the most radical reliance in the world; absolute reliance. It should not be hard to change your reliance from the shaky systems of Truth you have pursued, which have brought you little but disappointment—and the worship of personalities, to reliance on this glorious God-power. Step out on the Promises of God, and you will find that they do not need to be demonstrated, they will sustain you. Presently you go apart from them all, and go your way in silence and peace, giving thanks eternally to the Father. Do you begin to SENSE ME, the Christ-self, within you, as you read? And are you beginning to shake yourself free from the bondages of fear and limitation with which you have bound yourself? "Behold I make all (not some) things New." When this Christ-Power has come, *it* instantly neutralizes the human destiny, and causes man to function on the plane of Spirit which is not subject to the law of sin, sickness and death.

"Christ lives once for all. Christ reigns now and forever with you and in you and through you, and you are the reproduction of that identical resurrected

Christ, and through this Recognition you find yourself on "this" side of the cross. You are the resurrected Christ, not to return to the crucifixion and the cross any more. You are free. The resurrected life transcends gravitation of earthly laws and beliefs. It transcends lack, want and limitation, disease and all undesirable conditions."

It is so wonderful to know that the recognition of this Christ-self takes us to a point where the endless crucifying of ourselves stops. Nothing could be more wonderful than to meet with a group of souls who were not constantly in the throes of problems. Nothing could be more natural than an assembly of Christ Souls, who were above the gravitation of the human law which ceaselessly looks for a panacea for its troubles. The endless going through problems ends in death, disappointment and defeat. Many claim to be helped by their problems, yet the very one who claims what a tremendous advantage problems are, is the one who is constantly seeking to get rid of a problem, or to avoid it. When will we be honest with ourselves? We cannot get anywhere with the dishonesty of human mind, which, rather than admit its failure, makes some weak excuse to the world. Many failing to understand or apply the law, put on the garments of a martyr and go about complaining that they are being tried by the Lord. What for? Is the perfection of God helped by a soul being dragged through all sorts of evil? Does it make the water of a mountain stream any more pure and lovely if it be passed through the sewer of a city?

All this dishonesty of the human mind that has

failed to follow the Christ is laid aside in the new
revelation. What of it if you have made mistakes and
fallen, gone astray? The surrender to your God-self
has the instantaneous power to resurrect you. The
Christ on "*this*" side of the Cross is and was absolutely
free from what the world of human thought or belief
might try to do to him. And yet He *was* flesh and
blood, and ate and drank. It is wonderful! It is being
in the world and not of it. We begin to see that the
clarified consciousness would be the receiving station
of those new and higher laws which would make
miracles natural.

There is no half measure in the law of God. The
manifestation is not half-made; it is full and complete
and magnificent. The superstition of a thousand centuries falls as an old garment hoary with age, at the
Recognition of the Christ within. The fear and worry
you have gone through because of your superstitions
all disappear, because the new manifestation is receiving the glorious word of Life which is this side of the
Cross. The experience has been gone through. He
bore our sins for us and paid the price. When we
Recognize this we cease the sinning and partake of the
glorious reward that is waiting for us. Do you hear?
Yes—I AM speaking to *you*, the very one who at this
instant reads this line. Now—I speak to *you*. The
Christ has come nigh unto you. I AM waiting—let ME
into expression. Come and sup with ME. I know how
tired and worn-out you are with the years of seeking
ME in human doctrine.

"Be ye transformed by the renewing of your mind"
—the RENEWING of your mind prepares you to receive
the word which before was inaudible to you. The

renewed mind is now receiving the *living word* that
before could not be found, because it was hidden. It
is like the discovery of a new realm—it has powers
and laws that do not exist in the realm you have left.
New dimensions and capacities are possible to you. It
is wonderful! wonderful! wonderful!

*"From henceforth My Spirit will, in all ways and
means and phases of life, express My Mind in deed
and action."*

Dare you, you who read this wonderful statement,
"Go thou and do likewise"? This glorious statement
says in so many words that whatever the Spirit wishes
to do, that it can and will do through the Mind, in
deed and action. The end of doing things in the
spirit, and never seeing the manifestation, has come.

The true vision is not imagination, but is an actual
out-picturing of the thing in a concrete form. There
will be no more subtle twisting of the word to meet
the failures. The word shall *not* return unto *you* void
when it is spoken with this assurance.

It is astonishing we are told over and over these
wonderful things, and yet until we hear them with
the ear of spirit, we only get the emotion of how
lovely it would be *if* we could prove them. Never will
we be able to prove them until we stand at the point
of *absolute uncompromising acceptance.*

When Jesus said, after showing the marvellous
works, "Go thou and do likewise," do you suppose
He was jesting, or making fun of His followers? He
was speaking to "Thou"—anyone who would dare to
accept His God given heritage. And this voice, this
word, this command, is still ringing in the land, and

every once in a while a certain *"Thou"* answers, *"Yea, Lord,"* and finds that he is ready and willing to "Go thou and do likewise." Do you see how it stands for centuries and centuries as mere legend, and then all of a sudden out of the dead letter leaps the spirit of it into the Spirit of you? To-day the Word is again being spoken. All those that have ears will hear.

"That which is mine as the Son of the Living God will come to me by a way and through means that will not make it necessary to infringe on the rights of others. It will come without strain or soliciting, for I AM free from all barriers and free from all dishonesty and all appearances of dishonesty, for I Am here to prove the Supremacy of God in all expressions of good on the mortal plane. We are not seeking to get something for nothing. We are here that the works may be manifested in you and through you and by you and with you."

"As the gift of God is to you a free gift, you are the gift of God for the practical service of mankind, to be practical, to be of mental service to both God and man, as the concrete expression of God, endued with the power to bring forth the works of God, and to set aside the human limitations.

"How marvellous are Thy works, O Lord of Hosts." We are beginning to see the new way opening before us. It is through acceptance of the gifts of God—the unselfish acceptance of that power. Why should we wish to make it "Mine or Thine" any longer? It is not mine or thine, it is Christ's. We are merely partakers of the wonderful feast—we are eaters of the heavenly manna. We are revelators of the Word made flesh. Do you begin to see and *sense* the wonderful power that is given to you in heaven and on earth as soon as you ally yourself with this Inner Lord? It is easy and natural and needs no argument. It was, and is so simple that it is given to the child. Do you hear? You who read this line?

"The thing that is most essential is that if any one is of Me, he is lost in My Will, and he desires to be lost in My Will, and to be governed by My Spirit. Give Me your heart. By heart, I mean all of which your mental world consists; all the desires, the suspicions, the fears, limitations, the wishes and vain imaginings, the struggles and strain, everything, give it all to Me, and then when you have given all, if you desire to do anything or go any place, or be anything, that desire will be of Me, and its fulfilment will be certain and assured."

This complete surrender of the whole heart is the most wonderfully freeing process. Suddenly you realize, as never before, that the "Government shall be upon His shoulders." The government of your life, you have given it all over to the One power, and the management of everything is now under the law of harmony and bliss. A sort of Divine Fatalism sets in, which is so different from the human fatalism which sees only chaos at the end of its path. The Divine Fatalism that sets in is the assurance that everything is all right, and is coming out all right, because it is under the control of the Only Power. Beside this power there is no other, hence there is no interference—no obstacle, no fear or intervention—and the instant this is Recognized a thousand barriers of a thousand years are swept away from the path like so many strands of cobweb. Aren't you glad. Do you hear? You who read? Yes, *you* who read this very line. Relax your conscious mentality and all the striving and straining, and be at peace. There is no human combination of laws, no matter how time honoured, that can stand against the One Power when it is Recognized.

Do you see in the simple child-like giving over all your vain imaginings, of both evil and good, that you leave the avenue open wide for the expression of God? That is, you become an integral part of the whole, you are lost in the immensity of it all and the new and glorious plane of expression comes into view. In giving them all over, the "voice that moves upon the face of the deep" will reveal the completed and perfect thing awaiting your acceptance, and the hard labour is finished. "This is my beloved son in whom I am well pleased" carries with it something that makes it manifest to the Son as well as to the world.

"Whence cometh wisdom and understanding?" is the question asked in the Old Testament, and "where is her hiding place?" It is certain that she does not come from long study in the text-books of mankind, since the greatest savants have been those who have had little opportunity to study. We look to a Shakespeare for our model of plays, we look to the Greeks for art, we look to an unschooled Lincoln for our concept of diplomacy and humility. In fact, we look for wisdom anywhere but in the so-called archives of wisdom of mankind. Shakespeare wrote his wonderful plays and produced them without training of any sort, and yet we find not one coming from our best universities, who has spent years of study and research; able to write anything that compares favourably with Shakespeare's least play. Wisdom is that thing which comes into expression whenever it finds an open channel ready to express. Do you see how it is possible for you to accomplish the dream you have had for so long, in spite of the limitations you have built up about you?

"I have a way ye know not of." The I AM has ways and means that the human mind cannot conceive.

Inspiration will possess you and make it possible for you to suddenly arrive at the goal which you before desired, but saw as next to impossible. Do you hear, *you* who read this? *You* the poor worm of the dust, the one who never could do anything for fear and lack and limitation?

"Be not afraid—it is I"—the risen Lord comes to *you*—the freed expression of your Christ Consciousness comes into being.

THE FATHER-SHIP DEGREE

"The records *bear testimony of the fact that the Son ascended from the Earth plane to the Heavenly state of consciousness, to the Father.* 'Glorify me with the same glory I had with Thee before the world was.' *The Sonship degree, as an individual, was manifested nineteen hundred years ago. The Sonship degree has been Glorified, even in this age. It has been resurrected. It is making its ascension; its individual ascension in you. So you are now rising. Materialism actually crucified the Son; (the Sonship degree,) and it had to ascend to the Fathership Degree, which was above the beliefs in a law that could crucify.*

On coming into an understanding of the Truth, we are thrilled at first with the Power that is made manifest to us. We see all sorts of wonders performed, but, later on, we see that the one performing these wonders is not immune from all sorts of persecution and crucifixion. We are amazed to see that one in Truth with a good understanding has been figuratively put to death, maligned and run through with the swords of human belief, and not until the necessity of arising to the Fathership Degree was explained did we understand just what this persecution was. "He ascended unto the Father" is the part we have overlooked. We have hung on tenaciously to the Sonship degree. We have bound ourselves to the place where we must make wonders or demonstrations happen in direct opposition to human law.

In the parable we see that the Master of the vineyard, who went into a far country and left his vineyard in care of the servants, first sent his steward to reclaim the vineyards. The steward was destroyed. He then sent His Son and the Son came with all the authority of the Son, but they waylaid him and killed him too, although the Son was acting within his rights.

But what says the parable: "The Lord of those husbandmen will come and destroy those husbandmen, and give the vineyard unto others."

We see that the time has come for the Father-ship Degree to be Recognized and utilized. Jesus often spoke of the impossibility of doing anything without the Father, "The Father within, He doeth the works," and we realize that the Father-ship Degree is beyond the possible hurt or harm of the personal plane.

We hear of the Masters of India. It has been made plain there is only One Father, the Master of All. Any man can become conscious of this "Master," and partake of him in the degree he is willing to accept him. First as the Steward, then as the Son, and then as the Father. In the human plan of things the logical advancement of the Son is to the Father-ship Degree. He—so to speak—grows up and becomes a Father. This is only a glimmer of the process which goes on in consciousness. Having passed through the Stewardship Degree, and been beaten with many stripes, he advances to the place of the Son, and again is deprived of his heritage and thrown out of the vineyard, and is eventually murdered. At last he realizes the need of making manifest the Fatherhood Degree. The deep and hidden mysteries that are being revealed to you. Yes, to you the one who reads this very line.

"The human personality is being put out of busi-ness, and in the reign of the Fatherhood of God the vineyard will belong to the Father, and you then will be heirs and joint heirs with Christ, and you will drink the wine of inspiration anew in your Father's King-dom. Here and NOW we are beginning to drink of the fruit of the vine. It is wonderful! Joy beyond degrees, for it is written, 'I am the true Vine and ye are the branches. Every branch in Me that bringeth forth fruit he purgeth it, that it may bring forth more fruit.' We are in the kingdom NOW (you and I), and we are drinking this wondrous new Wine of Life NOW. We are drinking the Living Waters, which if a man drink thereof he shall never see death."

Yes, joy beyond degree, for the goal that you set before you ever so long ago, that of Mastership, is now possible through the process of losing the desire in God. When the will is lost in the Will of God, then it becomes God's Will, and that which the world sees as Mastership comes into the range of the possible. It is wonderful! And all for the simple acceptance of the Truth. 'Ye shall know the Truth and the Truth shall set you free" is again knocking at the doors for admission, and again a higher interpre-tation is brought out.

"Now are we the Sons of God, and it doth not yet appear what we shall be, but we know that we shall be like nim, for we shall see him as he is."

This admission that "it doth not appear what we shall be" is giving way before the new Revelation. We are beginning to understand that "No man shall see my face and live," and "But we know that we shall be like Him, for we shall see Him as He is," are true statements of the one individual progressing from the Sonship to the Fathership Degree. "We shall be like Him for we shall see Him as He is." As He IS, the present tense, and the here and NOW—not as He shall be, but as He IS now and always. And the works that He doeth shall be done through us because of our oneness with Him. It is wonderful!

"Realize that you are ascending as the Infinite or Universal Son, to the Infinite or Universal Father. Where you are Glorified with the same Glory you had before you left the Fatherhood degree. And here and now is the time. Therefore, you have nothing to fear. And this is it that was, or is now, exactly as was with the Sonship Degree, for the Son gave up His life (the Sonship Degree), and God raised up the Son and made Him both Christ and Lord to the glory of God.

In this new Revelation you will note the direct application. It speaks with authority. It tells you "do thus and so," giving with it the full word of authority and power to accomplish the same. We have been so long learning how—and have had so many lessons that had to be studied—that it is with a thrill of joy that we come to the place where the Voice speaks to us, recognizing in us the power and capacity to perform the words. The direct statement of what you are doing, as in the case of "You are ascending," is either true to you or it is not, in proportion to your ability to accept it at this instant. If you hesitate and begin to say how unworthy or unprepared you are, then it passes you by and will not come again until you rise and answer "Yea, Lord"—and accept the glorious gifts that you have been trying to demonstrate all these years.

If you confer with another it is pretty sure that some human opinions will creep in—the old process of trying to erect the Way to heaven by discussing it with another instantly brings failure, for you speak a different language from the start and cannot understand the confusion. Someone else may have a different opinion from yours, and it may be just different enough to keep you from grasping the chalice full of New Wine. I speak to you NOW—you will begin to hear this voice, and you, alone and by yourself, will begin to accept this glorious revelation. You will sink it deep in the Consciousness, and others shall see the light. But before the light is established, so many men, "whose breath is yet in their nostrils," will snuff out the new light. Do you understand? Are you afraid to "come to *me* across the Waters? Certainly the moment you look down to the human appearance you will sink in the sea of doubt and of human belief. Do you hear? I AM speaking to you. It is wonderful!

"Now just think of it, how marvellous it is to be lifted from materialism, from mortality to spirituality, to immortality. It is a wonderful blessing, for you will find that you are gradually lifted above the barrier and limitations of mortality and materialism. You realize that material things are controlled by Spirit, or the Divine Principle that is actually within them, and finally you come to know that the Material thing is in reality materialized spirit. And in that we rejoice because you have ascended to the Father, and been glorified with the same Glory you had before the world was.

This great union of the material and spiritual dispels all misunderstanding from the mind. Instead of trying to destroy matter, we begin to perceive that matter is merely Spirit materialized, and that it is operated by the Principle of Spirit. The great chaos in the universe has resulted not from matter being evil, but the misunderstanding of the Laws back of matter. Hence the confused laws have produced what to the human sense was chaos and discord, instead of harmony and joy. Confused wires on a switchboard will work great havoc in a city telephone exchange, and many wrong messages will be passed along which, if followed, would produce greater chaos and result in disaster. This homely illustration is a good picture of that which we see, the ugly pictures of sin, disease and death. The confused interpretation of the Principle back of Matter has caused us to set up a Kingdom opposed to God, in which, we claim, are living God-created beings, subject to every law apparently, but the God Law. Manifesting every sort of hateful discord—even to a futile human destiny, irrespective of God. Awake, thou that sleepest. The "Father" is taking us back to the condition that we were in before the World was. We are not patching up old conditions and bodies, we are beginning to reveal to ourselves the true creation of God; that which has awakened from the dream in a world operated by a power apart from God.

"If you, the followers of Christ, will walk worthy of your vocation wherewith you are called, you will behold the Life of Christ as brought into expression by Jesus. You will see this power through every avenue of life and through every adverse and undesirable condition or appearance, whatsoever it may be. It will be your guide, your saviour, your protection. It is indeed wonderful! Facts and figures too stout to be denied are established regarding the Truth that 'the Spirit, of the Consciousness of the Presence of God is the Source of all Supply and will satisfy every good desire. Therefore, I cannot be denied.'"

The point is stressed that we are to live exactly according to the teachings of Jesus, and many people think they have tried this in vain; but they have only been looking on that side of the teaching which they interpret as *overcoming*. They have not Recognized that they are to also live the joy, and partake of the heavenly manna and happiness as well. That the command to *Recognize* the Kingdom of Heaven as Here and Now is just as important as any of the other commands. The command to hear and obey in the face of evil is also important. The command to "Rise up and walk" is to be obeyed. And the command to partake of the heavenly manna and drink of the Living waters must be fulfilled. All these things we have looked upon as the rewards, but they are a part and parcel of the "Living exactly in accord with the teachings of Jesus the Christ."

Begin to realize that the Sons of God are entitled to the glorious sense of joy, of freedom and happiness, and they must begin to bring in this element of Praise, not with the hope of making something happen, but as a direct result of what they have discovered as being True. It is wonderful! Aren't you glad? You cannot help praising Him.

CLAIM YOUR RIGHT AND PRESS YOUR CLAIM

STOP looking for results. All the years you have been studying Truth you have spent a large part of your time looking for results, and have failed to find anything very gratifying. When the attention is taken away from the results, and put upon the power, then will the results be forthcoming. As soon as you seek God, not for the loaves and fishes but for Love of Truth, for love of the glorious Life, then all the necessary elements that go to make up this glorious Life, as pictured in the Garden of Eden, will be forthcoming. The anxious mind will get nothing. The person who is using Truth for results misses the glorious power and reason of all Life. It is as a child who eternally wants to know the answer to a problem and not the principle. If he is told the answer and does not know the principle, he has a temporary relief from his difficulties; but the next day the same problem may arise in another form with a slightly different answer, and he is lost again. If you will turn your attention to the Principle of this Wonderful Revelation, and make it Real and True to you by the process of Recognition, then will you find the answer before the problem. "Before they ask, I will answer," is the law of this principle.

So many things that you cannot understand now will be revealed to you. You will know what is in the expression of Infinite Supply. It is wonderful! One of the things that troubles many is why some people have such abundance, when they do nothing to get it and have all sorts of mean traits in their make-up. Wherever there is an aperture made, the Substance comes through into manifestation, and most of all, wherever there is an *unconscious* Recognition made, that is assumption.

This all seems very vague, but it is not. When you realize the One-ness you will understand why "All that the Father hath is mine" is true. All that the Father (your Christ Consciousness) has is yours when you become one with it, for you are then that consciousness. Through "your Father Consciousness" you are one with not only the manifested substance that we see in the world as dollars and cents, but you are one with the source of these symbols, you are one with the universe, and this one-ness gives you the keys to the infinite substance.

"The Spirit of the Consciousness of the Presence of God is the Source of All Supply, and will meet Every Need."

Note the word "all"—you are one with *all* substance, both manifest and unmanifest. Do you begin to see why you cease looking for symbols, and trying to make demonstrations? You are one with it all, with the principle back of that which gives the answer before the problem. "The eyes of the blind shall be opened." You have been blind. The conscious Recognition finally becomes the unconscious acceptance, just as you have an unconscious acceptance of your capacity to walk, or just as I am unconsciously accepting the fact that I am able to write this book. It is beyond thought, this acceptance—it is a taking for granted, very much the same as you take for granted that to-morrow will come, and it will, whether you recognize it or not. It is wonderful! Take God for granted, and you will find Him suddenly present within you and without you, and all about you. Just take for granted that the substance is all about you, but see that you tell no man. Show them, but not for love of display or to be known of men. You are one with the very minerals of the earth when you are one with this God-power, and when you take it for granted. Isn't it wonderful!

If you keep your *eyes* away from yourself and your personality, one day you discover that you have been born again. To be born again does not mean that you have all the old evil beliefs to be got rid of. To be born again is to come out new and fresh and glorious, with new capacities and new talents.

"I shall forget their back-sliding." The mistakes and faults that you formerly possessed, and the evils that you committed are forgiven because they are confessed and eliminated, and you have cleansed the temple and are free. One with God and one with everything in God's universe makes you immune from the so-called law of evil. It is wonderful.

"This is but the outer expression of the Mind within. It is the out-picturing of the fullness of the Abundance that I have in the Storehouse for the Souls of men."

The eyes of the blind are beginning to see into the storehouse, and perceive the infinite riches and abundance that are awaiting the coming of the *heir*. You have never tasted a per cent of a per cent of what is waiting for you when you make the glorious Recognition of the Presence. I do not mean a Presence of God and another. I mean when you come wholeheartedly and without *one* reservation to any lesser belief, and fling yourself into the depths of this Godpower. Let go, give up and blend yourself with the glorious Life-substance that will revive the desert of your life, and make the garden of Gethsemane suddenly become the Garden of Eden. The garden which lingers in your memory through all these years of weary wandering. It is wonderful! Do you begin to see the ease and the quietness of the coming of the Lord? "As the thief in the night," perhaps at the time when you are in the darkest state of consciousness. It is wonderful!

Yes, you must be glad—as *you* read these lines and as I write them to *you*—just to *you*—I am *standing* with the glorious agreement of gladness for *you*. Gladness and joy that floods everything full of light and beauty and causes *you* to smile, and bring you closer to the Realization, "God shall wipe all tears from your eyes—there shall be no more weeping." Do you hear? "God shall wipe all tears from your eyes." Tears are the sign of sorrow, and so if there is no sign of sorrow left there will be nothing left in your New Garden of Eden to make the sign appear. It is wonderful! wonderful! wonderful! "Heaven and earth are full of Thee." Beloved!

The petty human personality that has had to carry

on, and make itself known by its deeds; that thing which has been spreading itself like a silly peacock, and at the same time advocating the simple Christ, is disappearing from the scene of action, while the quiet, beautiful out-picturing of the God manifestation is taking place. It is wonderful!

The trying and struggling have ceased, and we find that the Power of God IS. Do you hear?— IS.

"I will cause you to walk in My statutes. I will put My action in you. I will walk in you. I will talk in you. I will run in you. I will express in you the glorious things that I have in the storehouse for you."

Some of the things that "Eyes have not seen and ears have not heard," that have not yet entered into the hearts of the demonstrators of Truth, shall be revealed to *you*, when you are ready to *see*. Do you hear? Things that have not been seen, and things that have not been heard. Laws and powers that the poor human mind cannot even grasp, let alone try to use. It is wonderful! You are beginning to see the wonderful glory of this new word. Things that have not entered into the heart of man. What are these wonderful things? Be still, you are grasping something that is between the lines. *Be still* (for heaven's sake) and be nothing, in order that I can make you everything. "If you lose your life (in My life), ye shall find it," but if you try to hold on to the pigmy personality that thinks it has done something, then you will finally be disillusioned. Another will come who will do greater works, and the mad mob of worshippers will turn from you and follow him. Do you see?

What if you did collect a few people together to

listen to your words about serving the Lord, and sacrificing to the Lord. Be true to yourself. Hypocrisy when recognized can be cast out. As if the Lord of all needed your sacrifice. The only sacrifice He wants is the sacrifice of the hypocrisy and the religious bigotry, and not the sacrifice of a good living. You have never yet seen any one in the *actual* service of the Lord begging bread (and this includes the begging for support of the Lord's work) or else the Scriptures are not true. What are you going to do about it? It is pretty strong meat, but be assured, beloved, it will build into you the new cells of life. When you are not afraid of being honest. If you are serving the Lord, you can rest assured that the WAY for that service is prepared for *you* without begging or getting around the truth with a sanctimonious play on words. It is wonderful!

Why not sacrifice your little works to the Lord? No matter how much you have done. Do not be afraid you will not get the credit. Let go—the only credit you want is the credit that the Lord gives those who serve Him. That is all that is worth anything. It is wonderful! "I came that your joy might be full." I said *full*—complete, pressed down and running over. Right here and NOW. Do you hear? *You* who read this page? It is wonderful! wonderful! wonderful!

"In the day of my power my people shall be willing," and wherever I go the people are willing. Why? Because he that conquers his own will is greater than he that taketh a city, and as "in Adam all shall die, so in Christ shall all be made alive."

We begin to see that not only the people are willing to serve you when you serve the Lord, but abundantly and gloriously, too, into whatsoever country or place you go. It will be so wonderful!

"Take your burdens to the Lord and leave them there. Take your little gods of belief to God and leave them there. It is harder for God to save a god of Gods than to save all the sinners in the world."

So, beloved, do not be a god of Gods. Do not be the little god that is running around looking for a personal following and praise. Give the glory and honour to the Father, and bear away the blessing of the Son. It is wonderful! Do not be a god of Gods. It is too bothersome, and your clay feet will sooner or later be dug out, and you will crash. It all seems to fall down upon us like drenching rain on dry lands.

God is NOW purifying humanity's understanding. "If your eye be single your whole body is full of Light." Do you hear? If you are seeing "One-ness," not a material universe and a spiritual universe, not a Jesus and a Christ but One-ness, then "the eye is single and full of light." The eye becomes single when you recognize "the spirit of the presence of the Consciousness of God is the Source of all supply." It is wonderful! *"God in you and God in Me will make you what you ought to be."*

The perfect agreement is between *us* Now, and it cannot fail to bring forth the fruits. Be still, do not worry. Do not try to set things right—just align your consciousness with God and then all will come right, and the evils will disappear. Anything is possible to God. Remember the things that "eyes have not seen and ears have not heard"—those wonderful things that the human intellect and learning have not had a chance to hash over, and tear to pieces and give out as sectarian doctrine. Aren't you glad? Well, some of this lovely unseen and unheard, and even unimagined, power is what is going to suddenly transform things for you. Quicker than your thinking and quicker than you can imagine, and in such a way that it will wipe out the memory of the evil that existed, until you will say, "Well, I was always like this," and that will be the Truth, for *you*, the Real Son of the Living God have always been "like that."

"God is your Father and you never had another. If you say that and accept it as true and then act as if some man was your father, then you are denying the Christ. I have declared this unto you. God is your Mother, and you never had another, and so God is your friends and your all."

The day of direct acceptance, radical acceptance of the word, has come. If you accept God as your Father as the Scriptures state, then from that time you should begin to act in this new manner. If you return to the human parenthood, you bring back with you all the limitations of that family and all the problems of a human birth. Do you see?

It is direct and absolute—it is "Yea, yea," or "Nay, nay." Either you do or you do not. If you accept it you can act in the manner that proves the sayings of the Lord. Step out on the promises of God, and see the glorious power of this new Recognition. It is wonderful! And so it is.

"Call no man your Father."

Look up your parents and see what kind of heritage you have, and you will understand the glorious power that is yours. You have been a prince of the Realm all the time that you were begging for a crust in the Streets of Life. Assert your God-power. Claim your own.

Pressing your claim in this instance is more natural and easy than in the human sense of claiming your rights and pressing your claim. You certainly have the right to life and all that goes to make up a life of harmony and joy, but try as you have, it has not been forthcoming. You have stood aghast at the success and fortune of some people. You have seen people born rich, who have every quality that would debar them from wealth in the human sense of the word, and also in the spiritual. Well, all this wonder is going to pass. Your new Father will take care of that.

Off the deep end of the diving board into the Ocean of Substance, all in at once and out into the Great Universal Deep of God's Love. You are not a bit afraid—how wonderfully the muscles of your new embodiment are working—how strong and easy you glide through, buoyed up by this great underlying and overlying and penetrating power of the Presence *Claim your right and press your claim*. What is your right! Think it over—take it, possess it—be it, live it, sing it into glorious expression of the here and now. It is wonderful!

ANOTHER DAY

"YOU are in another day—praise God. Christ in you is the victory. You cannot help being carried away in the Spirit. We have nothing to doubt, nothing to fear. A new heaven and a new earth are here. You have never been so happy before." My sheep hear my voice. Serve the Lord with gladness. *"The Divine Omnipresence lives, moves and breathes within you and has Its being in you."*

What will you do about it? What will you do with this Statement of Facts? Will you accept it, and take it with you into instantaneous expression? In the New Day we do not wait to have a withered arm rehabilitated by the long process of human healing and convalescing. In the New Day we discover that "whereas before I was blind NOW I can see." Right now, at this instant, as *you* read, it comes into expression without argument, without concentration and all the other man-made methods of doing things mentally. Right now, as you read and accept the truth as given you by the Father, can you see it into manifestation. Remember "I have a way ye know not of," and that is the *way* the new day is ushered in, and when *you* find yourself in a new day you find yourself in a *new consciousness* and in a renewed body and renewed

117

mind, in a gloriously transformed universe and yet somehow it is just the same.

What seems to be merely frost on the window-pane turns out to be a beautifully wrought design, so intricate and so beautiful that the human imagination is lost. It is wonderful! Do you understand what you see when "having eyes you see"? It is wonderful! You are in *another* day. Did you hear what has been said to *you*; no, not to someone else, but to *you* who reads this line? To *you* at this moment contemplating this page. "*You* are in *another* day." No amount of argument is going to make it so.

The so-called healing and changing of things takes place on the mental plane. There is nothing spiritual about them. You understand that Spirit could not be healed. God and His universe are above healing. The only thing that is being done is the mental is being changed, to be more in alignment with the realities of Being. It is wonderful! So *"Claim your right and press your claim."* First *be* it, and let your light so shine, to show forth your works to all men in thanksgiving and cheerfulness. Yea, in a wide open joy that cannot but spread itself all over the universe. That is praying without ceasing.

Be still—the floods of light that are coming to you are revealing to you the deep hidden things that eyes cannot see. Aren't you glad that you of yourself can do nothing? Aren't you glad that you have arrived at the point where: "I of myself can do nothing" is true? Isn't the soul of you singing? Singing like the caterpillar that lies hidden in the cocoon, when it contemplates the vision of its freedom.

Just cast your burdens on the Lord as you are told

and take a chance. Follow the wisdom that is being revealed to you within your own soul and be at peace. Let "the filthy be filthy still." "What is that to thee —follow thou Me." Isn't it wonderful! Are you beginning to glimpse the *NEW DAY?* We do not have to go anywhere to get there, for *I AM here, I AM there, I AM everywhere,* and I AM everything in every place at every moment of the day. It is wonderful! Can you open wide your consciousness and accept your God-given heritage?

Radical reliance and acceptance of the Presence of God. The more obstinate and impossible the human condition that envelopes you, the more glorious will be the revelation which will come through to you the moment *you* are ready to *believe* (accept) God as here and now. Talking about God and Heaven and all the lovely things does not make them real. Be still —*you* are beginning to see.

No condition can withstand the simple Recognition of this power. The strongest fortress of human belief will crumble like the walls of Jericho before a simple *WORD*, if that *word* is spoken with the authority of the God-given Power.

Christ in you is the victory.

"Two shall agree as touching on any point and it shall be established on earth." That is, it shall come into manifestation by the agreement which accepts it. It is interesting to know that the Agreement is waiting for *you*—no matter who *you* are, no matter where *you* are, for "*I AM here, I AM there, I AM everywhere*" at all times and under all conditions, and all *you* have to do is to make *your* agreement with the glorious revelation to see the *Victory* brought to your world. Brought into manifestation in the *NEW DAY*. It is wonderful! And so it is.

In the best philosophy we find it is necessary to know where to put a full stop, in order to save ourselves from terrible disillusionment. Have you already experienced disillusion by trying to go back and repeat something? You cannot go back to the state of consciousness you have left, and so it is well to know how and when to put the "full stop" to the past. "Let the dead bury their dead, follow thou ME."

You cannot help being carried away in the Spirit. I presume by now you do not want to "help" it. You are beginning to see that to "let the Mind of Christ be in *you*" is to experience some of the newer and more glorious things; and the feeling of being "carried away" from all the human limitations and bondage you have been fighting so long.

A battle that is fought after a war is over is the "*n*th degree" of folly. Well, do not commit any more folly. You have fought your long mental battle, the war with things is over.

When you "Put up your sword," that does not mean that you become a retreating coward; but that you are independent of the power that is represented by the sword. You have something that is infinitely more powerful than any material sword. Do you hear? You are a *shower-forth* of that which IS and *you* are a doer of the WORD—and you do not have to be burdened with any more bondage of personal doings. You do not have to take the blame or the credit for healing any one. God will be able to handle all that. Do you begin to Recognize that there is only ONE Power, and that we are not again going to divide it up into little parcels, called enemies, friends, healers, etc.? Just *one MASTER* with many and wonderful modes of expression.

"Why seek ye the living among the dead, I am the God of the living and not of the dead."

"You do not have to go down to the grave to find HIM. He dwells within you and is in you. God the Father is with you. The House of the Lord is lifted up. Fear not, be not dismayed. I AM your GOD, I AM with you, I WILL help YOU. I have done nothing yet in comparison to what I am going to do."

The great Impersonal Voice. "He that hath ears let him hear."

"Why seek ye the living among the dead." Why look farther in the dead letter for the Living Word? Within you lives the Word. You are the Word. *You* are one of the glorious *words* in the great anthem of joy, which is even now rising to the heights. It is wonderful! I AM a God of the Living and not of the dead." "Awake, thou that sleepest, and Christ shall give thee light." Awake, thou dead one, and come out of the tomb of your own making. "I AM a God of the living"—because God is LIFE. *"Claim your right and press your claim."*

"You do not have to go down in the grave to find Him." You do not have to go down into the grave in order to attain heaven. Beloved! this is all saying something to *you* that is too glorious to put into printed words. Do you argue—read for yourself the glorious thing that is hidden away, and be at peace, then will the soul of you sing for gladness. It is wonderful!

Don't you love the power of the words "Fear not, be not dismayed. I AM with you"? Seems as though everything you ever feared withers away and becomes dust. "Fear not, be not dismayed." Be not dismayed if I reveal to you, yes, to *you* who read this line, something that you have not yet heard or known, or something that you will never read, because there are no words adequate to convey the idea. Be not dismayed. "There are many things I could not tell you because of your unbelief." But now you are in a *New Day*, and just as soon as you are ready to hear some of these things, I will say them to you in language that you can grasp and understand. It is wonderful! Yes, it is wonderful that you have lived all these years on what I was able to tell you nineteen hundred years ago. The little that you did grasp has been all the real life and substance that you have had, but the things that I could not tell you then, are the very things that you most need to know now. Be still. I have a way ye know not. Do you hear? *You* who read this line? I AM speaking particularly to *you*.

"The mouth of the Lord hath spoken it." Do you want any other authority? All right, then, the bickering about what Mr. Blank or Miss Blanker said is of no more importance. I do not care what Mr. Blank said. I want to know what the Christ is saying within my consciousness right now. What the I AM said to Mr. Blank was for Mr. Blank. Do you see?

"I am so glad that a place has been prepared for you. The mouth of the Lord has spoken it."

So glad that a place has been prepared for you; that place in this state of consciousness, far above all mortality. You do not have to fear depression, hard times, or anything, for you are now on the plane of the New Day, on the level of consciousness to which you have suddenly arrived. "This is the 'place' I have prepared for you."

Do you hear? "I go to prepare a place for you" is just as important as any other promise. "*Step out on the promise.*" "I go to prepare a place for *you*," yes, for *you*, the one who reads this line. Then what is all this fussing about trying to prepare a place for yourself? "I go to prepare a place for you." Do you hear— when you get there the place will be waiting for you. "I go before you and make straight the way." It is wonderful!

"I Am the refuge"—in "Me are the cities of Refuge," and you do not have to make a hiding place against evil times. He that makes himself a place of hiding against the evil times will make that place a direct target for the enemy. He is the one that is broadcasting the fact that the evil is real, and that he is hiding from it. He is hiding from a material belief in another material belief.

He who runs into the Lord shall find the hiding place. Where the Lord is there is liberty. Do you see, then, that you are just as safe in the thick of the human battle as you are in the strongest dug-out? Are you making yourself a human target by advocating that people must run to a material refuge? It is wonderful to be unafraid out in the open fields with God. Do you hear?

"I go to prepare a place for you." All right—are you going to accept this place in consciousness, or the little shelter that someone is building, hoping to save your little human personality from danger? "Choose ye this day." Either God is All-Power or else there is another. If there be another then our preaching is in vain, futile and worthless. "Awake, thou that sleepest." God is your sure and absolute protection. Protection not only against the material machines of war, but of the human thinking machines that set up machine-guns of hatred and jealousy, and try to cut you down. It is wonderful! You are walking with Me, unafraid—"Though ten thousand may fall at thy right hand—ten thousand who prepared for evil and war—it shall not come nigh thee."

"I go to prepare a place for you, that where I am there you may be also." And where the Lord is there is liberty.

There is nothing to fear, for the Lord is round about you and in you and through you. It is wonderful! "Look again" is the command of the Prophet to his servant, who saw so many enemies and so much evil coming toward them—and the servant looked again, and, "Lo, the mountains were full of men and horses and chariots, and the words came, saying: 'Those that are for us are more than those that are against us.' " So, beloved, those that are for you are more than any aggregate mass of human belief, and so it is wonderful!

"You are a child of joy. You are in a New Day. You can sing your new song in the name and nature of Jesus Christ and it will go over. It will find its lodgment in the soul of that one who is ready to be helped out of the shell of human belief. If you address it to the Universe in the name of the Father, then will it

carry with it the glorious authority. It is wonderful.
Father, keep me in Thy love."

Do you hear? "You are a child of joy"—yes, I
know you may have read it a thousand times, but
I am saying something to you at this instant that will
touch the secret spring of realization, and cause you
to shout for joy and gladness. Not from the emotional
angle of human excitement, but from the deep wel-
ling up of the Spirit within you. Isn't it wonderful?
"Child of Joy." *You* I am speaking to—Child of Joy
in your New Day. Laugh; sing songs of gladness; you
are lifted up to the point of Being—presenting to the
Universe the glorious truth that you have at last
found the Father, and He is richly giving His love to
you. All the old adverse conditions and beliefs pass
away—you are in the *New Day*—it is wonderful, for
"God is your Father and you never had another"—so
"Claim your right and press your claim." Rejoice
and be exceeding glad for it is your Father's good
pleasure to give you the kingdom of Heaven—and
that kingdom is here and now.

THE LORD'S DOINGS

"This is the Lord's doings and it is marvellous in our eyes" (Matt. xxi. 42). Whatever it is—no matter what the appearance—you can know that the fullhearted, uncompromising statement that "This is the Lord's doings and it is marvellous in our eyes"—will instantly cause all worry and fretting to cease, and will bring out of the mist of human beliefs just what is the "Lord's doings" at that particular moment, and will cause the false appearances of evil to scatter into their nothingness, and make room for the perfect "doings" of the Lord.

You will shout "It is wonderful!" and will experience the thrilling sense of why it is wonderful. "This is the Lord's doings and it is marvellous." The wrath of man shall praise thee, and the evil of human thought shall bend its knee before the appearance of this God Power, right where you stand, in the identical place you are, at this moment, "This is the Lord's doings and it is marvellous in our eyes" will, if Recognized, cause you to see what has been going on all the while, hidden from your blinded eyes.

All the while you have been experiencing the dream of evil, the reality of Life with its glorious possibilities

is functioning on the other side of the thin veil, which
you rend when you can say in face of evil, "This is
the Lord's doings and it is marvellous in our eyes."
The veil is rent and the light pours through, and you
see that in reality it has never been any different. The
swirls of human belief pass off in the mist of forget-
fulness.

"This it the Lord's doings and it is wonderful in
our eyes." Realize this right in the face of the greatest
danger, or most evil-looking problem, and you will
defeat it, without doubt. "This is the Lord's doings"
is Recognition of the Presence of the Power, which
is active and working eternally into expression.

"This is the Lord's doings and it is wonderful in
our eyes."

*"Re-incarnation is only for the undeveloped and
imperfect. What need is there of re-incarnation, if
you are the perfect expression manifested? The perfect expression has no need of re-incarnating itself in
all sorts of characters, as it remains for ever. If you
will enlarge the borders of your tent, and let the Christ
Mind evolve in you, it will come forth into fruition,
and through the garments of human beliefs and character, will shine the True Self, perfect and free from
the limitations imposed upon you by the belief of
separateness."*

"This is the Lord's doings and it is marvellous in
our eyes." The Revelation is coming *steadily* through
into manifestation. We are beginning to see one veil
of human belief after another rent, and the clearer
and freer glimpse of the True Self is being revealed.

All the characters you have played before you found

your True Self, are as so many stage clothes which you have finally laid aside. Some of these costumes became so real to you that you have been bound to them, and have partaken of the nature of the character played, "Then through a glass darkly, but NOW face to face." Newness, holiness and freeness possess you. You are awakening out of the long night of sleep into the dawn of Reality. Something that transcends all the human doctrine is being poured out upon you.

The spirit of the letter is freed upon you. It is pouring over you like warm oil on a cold body. It is wonderful! Do you begin to see that the power of the word, when backed by the Recognition, will open the closed doors and give you the keys to the kingdom? What matter the past, birth, race, family or creed, the false education or the beliefs of a thousand generations? All of them go back into the box of imagination, which holds the stage props of former plays.

"*Being* HERE, *is coming to 'this' place in consciousness, whether you are in Europe, Asia, or Africa. It is to be lost in the Will of God, to be lost in the consciousness which says, 'Not my will but thine will be done.'*

"When your will is My will, then my will is your will, and the will of the Father is being done."

"*When you come to 'this' place in consciousness you have come to the place that humanity has been seeking through the centuries. At-one-ment with God means that you are wherever He is, for I AM here, I AM there, I AM everywhere.*"

Do you begin to see the wonder of it all, and the deep, secret teaching that is being poured out upon you? Secrets that are conveyed to you as *you* read, which no tongue will speak.

"He that hath ears let him hear." You do not have to prove it to someone else. When you are it *yourself*, that is enough proof. The light going from you will heal impersonally; thousands will touch *you* in life's way, and never know *you* by a human name, but shall be saved, changed, and healed. All of a sudden at your coming the healing will take place. The receptivity of that one in need will be filled by *your will* being one with the *will* of God; you will automatically be "about your Father's business."

"The Spirit of the Consciousness of the Presence of God will satisfy your every desire, for it is the creative force of all things and the source of all supply. Recognize this once and you begin to appropriate the gifts of God. You begin to experience the heirship to which Jesus referred."

Is there anything unnatural about being well supplied and taken care of? It is an automatic process between God and His Expression. It goes on without the benefit of prayer, begging or beseeching. It functions of its own accord. It is not called into action by any need, but is always in action, awaiting Recognition.

Once you let go the idea of a "static God," who only functions because you need something, you will incorporate into your consciousness the sanction of instantaneous *expression*. You will not have to wait for a prayer to be heard before results come into manifestation. You will begin to experience the instantaneous process of Recognition—"Before they call

I will answer"—because *I* have already answered. The Spirit of the Presence is always there, awaiting Recognition. Nothing is impossible to this Presence; nothing is difficult, nothing is hopeless. No matter how many human laws have to be set aside. With the coming of this Power the human troublesome thoughts are brushed aside as so many gnats. The atmosphere is instantly cleared. "This is the Lord's doings and it is marvellous in our eyes."

Do you not begin to see that this is so—that all the weary years of struggling with systems and ideas have passed out of the picture and the glorious effulgence of the Presence is filling everything full? "Believest thou this?" *You* who read this very line, at this very instant?

"*The Spirit of the Consciousness of the Presence.*" The Spirit is active and ready to make manifest the consciousness of the Presence. Those that have ears will hear the Word and partake of the heavenly manna, and be free.

Faith in things must go, in order that Faith in the Presence can hold forth. The continual sacrifice that is spoken of by the followers of Truth frightens many. "I have no pleasure in sacrifice—saith the Lord." The sacrifice of things is merely giving up the faith in the power of things. Until faith in the power of money is replaced by faith in God, the true everflowing substance of Life cannot come into free manifestation. Sacrificing the symbol and still holding on to faith in the symbol, is to find yourself without symbol or faith. Letting go of the love or the fear of money causes the infinite flow of substance to take place. "And he had twice as much as he had before" is the law of *letting go* of the love or fear of things. The moment you *let go* of a thing and come to the place where you can do without it, you do not have to do without it. You have simply got rid of the bondage of the fear or the love of the thing, and the thing can be used freely, and not use you. You are master of it.

This wonderful freedom from things gives you the infinite substance of all things. The manifestation of the right thing in the right place. Money is no good on a desert isle. Worshipping money as substance you fail to have the supply that meets the unique need.

"Isn't it wonderful, this Spirit of the Presence of the Consciousness of God, which is swallowing up everything; all lack, all fear, all evil, all the so-called human good, and giving you in place of it the satisfaction and the fulfillment of every desire. The fulfilment of every desire, when it is expressed in the terms of the Will of God, brings out the rightful expression, instead of the distorted human concept.

"This is the Lord's doings and it is wonderful in our eyes." Once you begin to *sense* the fact that God runs the universe, you relax and let the power express through *you*, and this relaxation is not physical inertia or inactivity, but a glorious going forth into manifestation. Nothing can stop it. Nothing can withhold it. No combination of human beliefs can withhold the glorious out-pouring of Spirit through you. Every thing you touch is filled with the power, every one you contact is made alive with the praise and glory of the Father—heaven and earth are full of the glorious freedom of the Sons of the Living God.

"The thought came to Jesus to command the stones to be made bread, and the thought came to Jesus to cast himself down from a pinnacle, and let people see what a wonder-worker he was. But the thought also came to Jesus that if he did such a thing he would be sidestepping the power and be using it for personal ends, and it would thereby be lost."

To many people the thought comes that if they can find out how to materialize money, or heal people instantaneously, they will have a big following, and will be considered holy men and doers of great works. They heed not the law. "Let not the right hand know what the left hand doeth."

What do you care whether a few hundred or thousand people are following you, and looking up to you? After all, these same people can turn and try to rend you at the slightest provocation. The Father has shown the serene way of being above all this personal worship, by actually manifesting God to such an extent that we are impartial and impersonal in our expression. What do you care whether a few people know that you have made a healing when, in the secret heart of you, you know that thousands have been able to see the light, and have gone on their way praising God—and not a person. If you know the power, it is evident you do not have to stand up and tell the people how wonderful you are, they will know it. The signs will always be present where the Presence is.

"All power is given unto *Me* in heaven and in earth" is a statement of a fact, but until you are ready to *Let* this power use you into expression, do not think for a moment you are going to lay hands on it. It is foolishness to think that the human selfish person you call by name is going to be made a steward of this magnificent power, and use it for the purpose of exalting himself and making a display of magic. "When you are ready *I* will do the works." Do you hear? *You* who read!

"Cast out of your system, by casting out of your consciousness, all prejudice, all bigotry, all fear, all condemnation, all denominations, all races, all colours, all families, all self, all flesh. Cast out all personal fancies and pleasures, and when you have cast them out of yourself you have cast them out of the only place they ever existed."

This seems like a life's work, but when you come by the way, the way of rejoicing, and Recognizing God as here, there and everywhere, it is easy and natural. You will see by the searchlight of your new-found God-consciousness. Your consciousness is *so* filled with the Presence, that the *automatic* house-cleaning takes place. The temple is purged of the dove sellers and money changers.

"When you shall have relinquished all of your pre-conceived ideas and opinions, fancies, pleasures, thoughts and minds, and all the tendencies that go with the personality of yourself, or your person, then Christ is ready to be revealed, for he is there waiting your sacrifice and self-denial, and he will arise and unfold himself in you."

All you have to do, Beloved, to have this glorious purging is to be honest enough to desire it, and then turn to the Father within and thank Him in Spirit and in Truth, and the Father, who seeth in secret, shall reward thee openly. No more is this a vague promise. It is something that you can fulfil instantly. "Believest thou this?" "Thank you, Father," is the glorious Recognition of the Presence of the Power. "*I am here, I am there, I am everywhere,*" and So It Is.

"This is the Lord's doings and it is wonderful in our eyes."

"The Father, Son and Holy Ghost are One. Your Mentality, your Personality and your Physicality become one with your Spirituality."

This glorious One-ness is the perfect wholeness of which the Bible speaks. *"Be ye whole."* When the idea of one-ness possesses you, then there is not *another*. There is, then, nothing to harm, hurt, destroy or combat. Do you see the perfect peace that comes from this glorious union?

What you are in Spirit you are in the physical— all the glorious freshness and agelessness of spirit is presented to the physical world, because of this union. A camera plate, holding a lovely picture, in the dark, is brought into contact with a tray of developer and instantly gives up the hidden thing. So your body will bring forth the glorious hidden picture of the Son of the Living God, will reveal that which was always there, since the beginning, since the moment you were created in the image and likeness of Him.

"You do not have to think about to-morrow. It is in the keeping of the Lord, and it is wonderful. The Truth will set all the prisoners free from their super-

stitutions, free from lack, free from want, and all limi-
tations; and finally you, as an individual, will come
out from under the earth's gravitation—the gravita-
tion of thoughts of evil, fear, loss and limitation. You
are free indeed."

After the Recognition of God as present, the Scripture, "Take no thought for the body, the purse, the
scrip, the way," etc., becomes literally and practically
true, and this taking no thought is filled with Recognition and thanksgiving for the Power made manifest
to us. Everything we need is supplied; everything
we must have is instantly forthcoming. Believest thou
this?—*You* who read. It is so written in the Scriptures
—can it be that the Word of God is false, and that
His promises are not fulfilled?

"The birds of the air have nests, and the foxes have
holes, but the Son of Man has nowhere to lay His
head."

This shows the freedom of the son—he is not bound
by possession, he is constantly in possession of all
wherever he goes—he has the consciousness of the
"Upper chamber, the robe, the scrip, the purse,"
etc., he is not bound to anything. He is free and abundantly supplied. The consciousness of anything will
reproduce itself anywhere; so if you really have a consciousness of a home, no matter into what locality you
go, that consciousness will be out-pictured and made
manifest. The same thing is true of all the other gifts.
Once you accept the Gift, the manifestation of that
gift comes forth anywhere. The symbol may be used
or destroyed, but as long as the consciousness of the
Accepted Gift remains, the manifestation will be

forthcoming whenever needed. It is wonderful. Aren't you glad.

"This is the Lord's doing and it is marvellous in our eyes."

IMPERSONAL LIFE

"CALL NO MAN your Father upon the earth; for one is your Father which is in heaven." "*Be the same as though God were right here with you. God is your only Father and you never had another.*"

When we are absent from the body we are present with the Lord, and when we are absent from personalities we are present with the Christ, and we hear with the ear of Spirit. Until the eye has become single and the ear has become single, we will eternally be fastening on to a material basis the things we hear of Spirit. This particular thing was what made Jesus the Christ appear in such a distorted light. His continued effort to make a man see that everything He said about Himself was also true of the auditor, was in most instances turned against Him. But to-day anyone who claims to be like Jesus meets the same sort of rebuff and scorn. And so we learn to place the seal upon our lips and let joy be full, because "I came that your joy might be full." Do you hear? It is your business to see that you get the full measure of joy right here and now. Never mind what anyone else has to say. The Spirit has spoken to you and said "I came that YOUR joy might be full," and if it is not full, it is because you are not minding your own business, but are looking to some outside source for your joy. If you are "about your Father's business," you are full of joy and accomplishment, for it cannot be otherwise. The diligent soul will mind its own business. Do not be busy setting other people right, lest you find yourself in the wrong and have much to undo. Isn't it peaceful and quiet in this place of letting others alone?

"Only when the seal is on your lips and you go within to the ME of You, and identify yourself with this, can you taste of the glories of the kingdom."

"Let your moderations be known to all men that the Lord is at hand." "Let" this take place just like you are going to "let" your light so shine. It does not say to "Make" your moderations known to all men. They will be known the moment you *let* them. By identifying ourselves with the Power we become like it, and are actually *it* because what you are one with, you are.

"I advocate the Kingdom here and now. Glorify yourself in Heaven. Take all you want, but be sure to get the best. When you have cancelled all your preconceived ideas, then shall you live for ever. All that you have to do to have eternal life is to 'Know Me.' "

Do you see that which lies before you in the glorious way to heaven through heaven—all heaven, even the way to heaven. And all alone and yet with the

infinite hosts of Heaven. I have many things to say
to you.

*"Christ in you and Christ in me will make the
whole world what it ought to be, and from every
undesirable condition set you free."*

The perfect agreement between you and your soul
will release you from the bondage of a divided
world, where two powers are constantly warring one
against the other.

*"I know that the Earth is the Lord's and the full-
ness thereof, and they that dwell therein, but still I
will not usurp any authority by taking that which is
not freely offered."*

While "all that the Father hath is mine," yet the
perfect gift if offered to me, and I do not have to go
outside this glorious law to attain mine. The man who
does this in a material way becomes what the human
thought calls a robber. He may pass a bank and declare that "all that the father hath is his," and proceed
to appropriate it, but he is operating on a double
standard basis. Until the eye becomes single and the
ear becomes single, the Light that is necessary to appropriate the infinite gifts of Spirit does not come,
and the attempt to enter Heaven by violence is met
with self-imposed resistance. Do you see? Do you
understand why the only thing needful is to make
this glorious union between the Father and Son, and
to assume the "Body" of Jesus Christ, the resurrected
body—the whole and perfect body of flesh and bones,
which was not subject to any of the human laws
which operated over "flesh and bones"?

"In God we trust" is stamped on most of the American coins, yet until this becomes true, the individual has his trust in the symbol, and not in that which is back of it, and the power is again divided; he experiences all sorts of false laws that operate over the symbol, none of which operate over that which is back of the symbol. Do you see? Do you hear? You are beginning to see something. Saying; "I have put my trust in God for my supply," does not mean anything. You do not have to wait if you have. The helpless attitude of the martyr does not acquire any manifestation of the power, from God. The prodigal lay in his self-created filth, and would still be lying there, if he, himself, had not arisen and gone to his Father. He had to recognize that he first had a Father before he could rise. So you first have to recognize that you have something in which to put your trust before you can see the symbols of this trust manifest to you. It is wonderful!

Recognition of the Presence is always accompanied by joy. "Come before His Presence with joy." "Make a glad sound." "There is joy in the presence of Angels." "Enter into thy joy," etc. There is no night there—in the There of this Recognition there is no night of limitation or grief. Nothing that you have missed, or left, or given up or had taken away from you in the human sense can compare with the outpouring that is about to take place by this new Recognition, and this time it is to be the materialization of the Spirit in such a way that it will be real and tangible.

Human intellect is going to find it all so stupid, and so does it find the idea of actually trusting in God for all substance foolish; but it does not find the symbols that come into manifestation that way so stupid. "So be still and know that I AM God."

"Take all you want, but be sure you get the best."

"You cannot expect to have My Spirit unless you have My Mind, and you cannot expect to maintain My Mind unless you have My Love. You will so vividly gaze upon this Presence by the Recognition and the wholeness of your Mind, that you will reproduce and manifest Him in your daily Life, not only in your Life but also in your Flesh. Christ manifest in the flesh will save you from death."

"Be ye transformed by the renewing of your mind." How can you expect to have the Spirit or Life of this glorious power unless the mind is transformed? Unless you have recognized the Presence here and now, and assume the glorious gifts of the Spirit. "Glory to God in the highest—peace on earth, goodwill to men." Just as you have already accepted your Lord—your inner lord, and begun to accept the gifts from Him; just so you will continue to enlarge the borders of your tent. You will launch out on to deeper waters. You will learn more and more to be absent from the body and present with the Power. A man who consciously drives a car is not nearly as capable as the one who drives automatically, though both of them may be just as present in the material car. To be absent from the body is to be present with something that is higher in its operation than any of the so-called laws of muscle and nerve with their limited capacity, and when you begin to understand this you will see that the power is greater than the instrument through which it expresses.

"The truth of My Organization is the Kingdom of God. Not from an organizational standpoint, but from a Spiritual standpoint. It is the Kingdom of God."

The pure teaching of the Christ without form or creed leaves one free and untrammelled to hear the *inspired* word of God anywhere, for anywhere is the Kingdom of Heaven when you know it.

"When we are conscious of God's presence, when we are conscious that God is with us at all times and in all places, then *the Spirit of that Consciousness is the source of all supply and it satisfies every good desire.* That is Absolute Truth. When mankind comes to this point of acceptance of the Presence, then the great burden of human laws drop from him. They no longer exist as a reality. 'Come unto Me all ye that labour and are heavy laden and I shall give you rest' is something that can be actually experienced."

Yes, I know, some are going to say, "that's where the rub comes in." "WHEN"—that is what we have been trying to do for ever so long. The reason we have failed to do it is because we have TRIED to do it, instead of just doing it by the process of Recognizing the Presence here and now. A child can do it, we are told, and presently we find that we can too. And joy of joys, we are actually doing it, and the least thing is not too small, and the greatest thing is not too big for the operation of this glorious Revelation. Watch, watch, watch. I said the least thing is not too small. Do you let the little things slip up on you. Just consign everything to this Power. Just cast every little thing over on this Power, and bear away the great blessing of Spirit Now. Everything that seems impossible is just the thing to place under this power. The more difficult the human sense says it is, the more wonderful will be the solution. Put the seal on your lips—be still. Do you hear?

"Call upon Me in the day of trouble, and I will deliver thee."

"Call on the Christ in everybody. Call on the Christ in anybody who is in trouble, and God will respond. That is your point of contact. Speak abstractly but surely to the Christ in them, as the Great Love Master did to Lazarus. He called the Christ in Lazarus to 'come forth.' If the one you are helping seems to be in the most dangerous and critical condition, call on the Christ in them, and the Christ in that individual will respond."

The old idea of treating a sick man, or a dying man, or a poor man is set aside by the way the Master gave to us. "Call upon Me, and I will deliver you." Addressing the Christ is not an effort to heal the sick man, so much as it is a pure Recognition of the perfect manifestation that is there all the time. Calling on this perfect manifestation in perfect confidence assures results. We look through the surface reflection to see the bottom of the pool, and we look past the surface beliefs to see the reality of being. Are you afraid to "Call upon Me in the day of trouble?"

"Just what you can ask God for, that God can give to you. There are few people radical enough to believe that."

"The things that are material are Spiritualized, and the things that are Spiritual are materialized, and

heaven and earth are one, and the Kingdoms of this world have become the Kingdoms of our Lord."

Are you one of those Radical people who are through with all this talk about the Truth? Are you "fed-up" with words, affirmations, systems—ways and means; and are you coming to the point of departure which will take you back to the teaching of Jesus Christ without brand, diploma, trade mark or system? With this new and wonderful One-ness of soul and body—of Jesus-Christ—you can open the Book anywhere and find the message, speaking to you with a new tongue because your ears have been unstopped and your eye is single to the All good of God.

"You are healed! You are HEALED! You ARE HEALED! YOU ARE HEALED!! It is wonderful! wonderful! wonderful!

The great flood of light that is pouring over you, flooding you with healing—with release from a hundred and one little worries and cares—is the oil of joy that is being poured on to your head. You are anointed with this precious oil because you have Recognized the Presence, and you can hear the above words spoken directly to you. It is wonderful! wonderful! wonderful!

"Take the name of Jesus with you. Take this Mighty name with you wherever you go. Take the name of your Father with you wherever you go, child of Joy, Life, Health and Love. It will in Joy and comfort keep you. Take his Mighty name with you wherever you go. If you are in any way doubtful, afraid, uncertain, just take this blessed name with you

*and feel, 'Thank you, Father, it is wonderful,' and
you will see that what I said to you, 'call upon Me
in the day of trouble and I will help you,' is true and
everlastingly true and usable."*

The great releasing power is spoken into manifestation through the name of Jesus Christ; through the
Nature or Presence of Jesus Christ—the materialized
Christ and the Spiritualized Jesus state of consciousness, in which you are now functioning.

*"You are in another day. You are not in the old
day. You are in the day of our Lord. This is no
longer a man's day, but it is the day of our Lord.
Therefore, no adverse winds of doctrines, and ideas
and opinions, can any longer stand in the presence of
God, for God is a consuming Fire, and has come to
purify the world."*

Man with his heavy learning and foolish intellect
has had his day. "We are NOW in the Lord's day"—
and likewise we are in the Year of our Lord. It is
wonderful! If this is the year of our Lord, then it is
not full of all sorts of unexpected evils and fears. This
is the Lord's year, and it is not subject to sun, moon
or stars. The Lord, He is one, and His kingdom shall
He not give to another. You are in another day. You
are in the year of the Lord. Do you hear?

*"God has been just as operative for the souls of the
children of men without a body as with one. He has
the way that you know not of. It is wonderful, this
Impersonal Life—this one-ness of life."* He who seeks
to save his life shall lose it, and he that shall lose his
life shall find it in the infinite Impersonal Life of God.

THE GLORY OF GOD

THIS IS THE DAY when men speak of Rays. The
Scientific world is full of rays— the Cosmic ray, the
Violet ray, the Light ray, etc., etc. The emanation
of light substance from a body of light or a centre
of light. And now comes the "Glo-ray," the Ray
of light emanating from God. It is wonderful! In the
simple word "glory," which has always been more or
less vague as to meaning, we find the clear lucid explanation. "*The Glo-ray of God*"— the flood of light
that comes from God—and in the same sense the word
"Glorious" might be interpreted as a great fan of rays
emanating from the Centre of the Universe. The
word "glory" is always connected with a flow of
light and illumination.

"*Every one of you can rise and shine NOW, for
your light has truly come and the Glo-ray of God
has risen upon you. God has 'rayed,' as it were, his
light upon you. The glow of God's rays are upon
you. The rays of light—of the sun-light of Life—have
been rayed upon you. It is wonderful! God in one
man is a majority. You are experiencing the Glo-ray
of the only begotten of the Father.*"

The glowing life substance which has been obscured for so many centuries, hidden beneath an avalanche of words and teachings is at last freed and "he that hath eyes shall see." Do you begin to see? With the coming of this glory into your life the hidden things are revealed, and you perceive the kingdom here and now in this glorious effulgence of illumination that is now upon you. Do you hear? I said that is NOW upon *You?* It is written to *you, so* that *you* may read and run, and run and read. It is the great Revelation that comes to *you* and makes you exclaim "whereas before I was blind, NOW (right this instant) I can see." It is wonderful! As you read you are experiencing the new light of understanding. Did you hear? I said *you.* Yes, *you* who read this line.

The simplicity of it all baffles us. Are you going to read it all over, then think about it and then try to put it into practice? That is what you have been doing for years. I am speaking to you right now—I want you to open *your* eyes with the same ease that the blind man opened his eyes. At that very instant he was spoken to. I AM speaking to you *now.* The blind man obeyed because he experienced the *Gloray,* as the only begotten of the Father. "Full of Light and Truth."

Now is your chance. Now it has come to *you.* Now with the same ease and mastery that was given to *you* in the beginning, you can open *your* eyes and see Now *you* can stretch forth your withered arm (withered power) and claim your own, for the "*Gloray of God has risen upon you.*" Now. The old universe of human thinking is tumbling about *you,* it is all passing out, so that the new creation—the new heaven and the new earth—shall appear. Appear to whom? To *you?* It does not make any difference whether anyone else sees it or not. When *you* see it yourself, you will find plenty of souls who see it likewise, and who are singing the song of gladness, for the *Glo-ray* of God has risen upon them.

The new heaven and the new earth—the former heaven and former earth that you tried to demonstrate into perfection—are passing away, and the new heaven and the new earth are coming into view.

"Out in the field alone with God. It is wonderful! For the people there struggling in darkness have seen a great Light. It is the Glo-ray of the Presence that causes the Light. You have never seen such a ray of Love before in all your life, as you are now prepared to see, the Glory of HIS Love."

Heaven and earth are full of this *Glo-ray* of God. The air you breathe is charged with the glorious Light Substance. The unseen-seen power of the ray that instantly makes manifest the perfection "His flesh was new and fresh like a child." Can you imagine that happening through any process of the human mind or of demonstration? Do you see the New Heaven that is descending within you, and bringing this glorious light of understanding? Can you be other than glad? *You* who read this line?

Come unto ME all ye that hunger and thirst; all ye that are sick and fearful; all ye that are tired and worn out with life; and I shall give you rest. It it wonderful! Plunge into this glorious effulgence of Light, and free yourself from the dirty human opinions and beliefs. "Call upon me in the day of trouble and I will answer you"; do *you* believe this is the truth? If so, you must believe that the "Me" is greater than any trouble you can possibly imagine. The invitation is made, indicating that immediate help will be given, so the Power is greater and more potent than any supposed human power.

Step out on the promises of God, and be freed from the false human laws that have been holding you in bondage for all these many years. *Glo-ray* to God in the Highest, peace on earth, good will to men. Good will to everything and everybody. Good will to *yourself* and *your* poor tortured body and universe. Good will and *Glo-ray* to the entire universe.

You can safely declare that the Kingdom of Heaven is at hand. I did not say *argue* that it is, or theorize that it is, or listen to a lot of talk about making it come to pass. I said *you* can declare to the world that the Kingdom of Heaven is *here* and *now*. Do not bother about whether they take it or leave it—you have given it to them, and sooner or later they will awaken to the fact that the Bridegroom of freedom has passed along and gone into the City to the feast. Do not *argue*. Truth stands supreme. It is now here and present, and needs but to be Recognized to be made manifest.

"Aren't you glad that something came along and cleaned you up? It is wonderful! Cleaned your heart and cleaned your mind, and cleaned your body. Now you can see Him as He is, and can tell the story, 'Saved by Grace.' Aren't you glad? There are many things I could say to you, I AM here, and I AM there,

I AM everywhere. 'When I am absent from the body I am present with the Lord.' "

When you are absent from the embodiment of your human ideas, you are at that instant present with the Lord—that is, you are one with the Universe, and you have escaped the limitations of the personality, and the laws and bondage that hold for the personality are no longer a part of your universe. It is wonderful! Little by little the light is coming through and the new day is dawning. "*Step out on to the promises,*" and keep your eyes open to the new idea, and *you* will be able to walk over the waves of human belief, and safely arrive at the boat wherein your Master waits.

I know that this means something beyond declaring the Truth. It means an outright acceptance of the Word of God. In its entirety—in its instant usableness. It means the putting out of a withered arm to find it restored and whole; it means opening the eyes that were blind and instantly seeing the Glory of God. It means taking the piece of gold from the fish's mouth. It is wonderful! "My Glory will I not give unto another." I shall be wise as a serpent and harmless as a dove. I shall be dumb as lambs before the slaughter. It is better to let the wise ones argue about it—you just begin to *Be* the thing—you just begin to appropriate your good and keep still. Your stillness will be more powerful and more heard than the clamouring of a thousand. Do you hear? *You* who read this line. "In him was the light, the light that lighteth every man that cometh into the world."

"Aren't you glad that it lighteth EVERY *man instead*

of SOME *men? You are the Light of the world, your world; and when you Recognize this, your light is lost in the universal Glory of God. All you need to do is to let the Glow rays through into expression. Let them Glow—let the rays of God 'glow' you, and let the 'Glows' of God ray you out into expression. Aren't you glad? It is wonderful! I say the 'glows' that are lighting every man (not some) to salvation. The Glow of the Rays will be a light upon your path. I will light up your pathway, for as I am, so are you— if you only know it."*

Do you "know it," and are you going to accept this glorious in-flood of light and be still, or are you going to *try to know it?* The "Be still and know that I AM God" used to be interpreted by physical stillness, while the mind busied itself with a thousand and one arguments about knowing itself to be God. But the net results have produced nothing tangible. Now the *new* consciousness of the *knowing* is so close to *perceiving something* as real, that words and human thinking ceases—and man beholds the *Glory* of the only begotten of the Father. How many times must *I* pass you on life's highway, and speak the Word to *you* and be turned aside? When will you stop looking for me in the robe of a Teacher or a Master, and perceive me at I AM? Do you see? Are you experiencing this *"Know"? "You are the same as I AM —if you know it,"* if you will accept it and take your good and exclaim to the world "Thank you, Father." No wonder the Master said, "I thank you, Father, that thou hast revealed this unto babes, and withheld it from the wise and prudent." The wise and prudent have toyed with the Word long enough, and they have only an archive full of dusty words and letters that are dead and without life. But you have been born again and are new and free. You are the *"child"* in consciousness. Not childish nor infantile, nor credulous, but fine, clean, untouched in consciousness, not confused with human learning of evil and false laws. You are, therefore, ready to accept, appropriate to the babes, but not to the wise and prudent. This is written unto you again, Beloved! Do *you* hear? "And of his fullness have we received grace for grace."

Grace is that which transcends the working of the human Law. "My grace is sufficient for thee." The Grace of this glorious power is sufficient. Be still, it is sufficient for *you*, and will carry you through the darkest night of human belief, right out into the Glory of the Presence. The scales shall fall from your eyes and you shall perceive the New heaven and the New earth—here and now.

Everybody—yes, every one, has received the Grace for Grace, the redemption, whether he be conscious of it or not, and as fast as *you* become conscious of the Presence, just so fast do you perceive the here and now of the new idea. Old things have passed away. "Behold I make all things (not some things) new."

As the Light of this Glory dawns upon you it will light away all the little habits which have been so troublesome. One false desire after another will fall away from you. Not through the method of condemnation or fighting, but through the power of redemption that comes in this Glory. It is wonderful! As the Light "glows" you into expression others will see the light which is not made to shine, but which is LET to shine, and in that light will they be able to discover the Glory that is theirs, and has been theirs since the beginning of the world. You, *you* who read this line. The mist of your fear has been dispersed, and you see the sunlight of the New Heaven and the New earth upon you.

"Ye are the light of the World (your world). A city that is set upon a hill cannot be hid. Christ said: 'Ye are the Light of this World'—you have as much right to this light as anybody in the world. When you claim your heritage of Light, then you will live it and be it, no matter how far you have travelled into the darkness of human misunderstanding. Do not go about any longer drunken with the Spirit of Babylon, that is, do not go around drunken with the spirit of the mysterious Babylon, that is fallen. Do not go around with her that has made all nations drunk with the wine of her fornication, but let your Light so shine. Let this unseen-seen power perform the miracles that the human sense marvels at so much. I hope you will take this in—the glow that God has rayed on you."

The darkness of human misunderstanding is all there is to your problem. There is no darkness in the Presence. It is the misunderstanding of the human mind. In reality, there is no understanding in the human mind, it is founded and established on a pack of false beliefs that it takes as a basis, and which it discards almost hourly for new discoveries. But the foundations of Truth shall not pass away nor change, they are eternally fixed and rest for evermore in the bosom of the Father.

"He shall gather the good wheat in His garner, but the chaff shall He burn up with unquenchable fire." The coming of this Glory will utterly destroy the power of human beliefs—it will burn up the chaff of human thinking and garner the pure wheat of Truth into the storehouse. "Thou re-storeth my soul," the soul that has been scattered over many beliefs shall be re-stored, shall be stored up again, and in this re-union shall be the great strength of the One. Why do you worry and fear? Everything is all right with you, for the "Mouth of the Lord hath spoken it." Do you hear? You who read this line.

"Let the light (the Glory) emanate from you, and as you go your way men shall be healed and helped by this silent, glorious, unseen touch of light.

"Do not go around with the spirit of Babylon." Do not go further with the babbling crowd, who are more interested in the personality and the personal life of a messenger than his message. Just so sure as you find the curious Babylonian seeking the messenger and not the message, you can withdraw from that presence, for you are with the one who will make you drunk with the wine of her fornication. Be still, and know. It is well. It is wonderful! Do not try to build the tower of Babel. They want to build a tower high enough to reach heaven, not realizing that heaven is right where they are, and not in the skies of their imagination. Do you see? Do you hear? You do not have to build the Kingdom of Heaven. It is already established, you have to accept it and live in it and make it your home, here and now. But each must enter by himself. You cannot lug some unwilling soul into heaven, however much they may

mean to you. You thought that you must help them in, bind them fast with the false laws of weakness. Who are you to say just how far they have come? Have a care that you yourself may not fall into the ditch you are digging for them by seeing them eternally as weak, and unable to appropriate this glorious God Power.

THE PLACE PREPARED

"I GO to prepare a place for you, that where I AM there ye may be also."

Already this Recognized "I AM" has gone to prepare a place in consciousness, so that the body may be there also. So that the body and soul may at last be one. The I AM has gone to prepare a place for you. Having Recognized this Presence as God within and without you, then the way through the dense beliefs of matter as separate from Spirit must be made, and the débris cleared away. The I AM has gone ahead and is doing this on the unseen. Unconsciously NOW many things and conditions are being wiped out before they have a chance to show themselves as beliefs, so in the Secret Place beliefs are destroyed before they have an opportunity to come into manifestation. If the bud on a tree is destroyed when it first appears, it saves hacking and tearing away at a fearful branch later on. So the I AM has gone to prepare a place for you. A place in consciousness where the body will have caught up, as it were, with the I AM. Where the Jesus-Christ shall be one in mind, soul and body.

"And if I go, I shall come again and receive you unto Myself." Fret not if you find yourself standing

159

alone for a moment—"I shall never leave you." "And if I go, I shall come (into manifestation) again and receive you unto Myself." I shall be wedded to the body. I shall become one with my manifestation. Soul and body will no more war one with the other, but shall come into perfect union. The great cleansing of the temple has been the breaking up of many beliefs and faiths. Everything that can be broken must go anyway, so fret not. "I will never leave you"—the I Am, though it may seem to have gone from you, is there in the unseen all the while, just as the image is on the exposed negative, although you do not see it.

"I go to prepare a place for you." I go to make ready the new state of consciousness that must come into visibility. Always we have talked of states of consciousness as something unseen, but the day of this mentally living in heaven, and physically dwelling in the hell of beliefs and adverse conditions is over. That which is true in consciousness must have its material counterpart, when the two become one. No more dwelling in the imaginary heaven where all is right, and actually existing in a realm where everything has to be set right daily. Can you see that the "Word must become flesh" and dwell among us, and then the "Answer appears before the problem"? Aren't you glad? It is wonderful!

The moment the consciousness knows and actually accepts a thing it is instantly out into manifestation. That is the state that Jesus spoke of and knew existed —that was why, when He had a consciousness of substance, it came out as gold, wine, bread, fish—whatsoever was needed at that instant.

Do you begin to see the change that must come? The change—an escape from the dual world into which we have again fallen. Long ago we talked about a spiritual world and a material world before we ever heard a word of this Truth, and when we discovered the truth, we thought we had something different, but in the end we found that we still had the same imaginary heaven, and the real earth full of evil to overcome. It is not so very different from the orthodox heaven and earth after all. This is the heaven and earth which must pass away, so that the New Heaven and earth may appear. Do you begin to see how this emptying-out process of all systems, creeds, cults, teachers, books, etc., had to take place? "They have taken my Lord away." No; already you are finding this emptiness is the glorious place that is being filled with the new reality of Spirit, which will concrete its manifestations without the thin excuses of the mortal mind.

I know you are tired of consoling yourself every time that you have asked and failed to receive, with the asinine reasoning: "Well, it is not best that I have that now." What a bitter pill to swallow, but it is a drug that excuses the failure to understand, and apply the principle of this glorious Truth.

No matter—"there is *now* no condemnation to those who are in Christ-Jesus." It does not make any difference what you have done—how many beliefs you have accepted and tried to function; how many times you have failed. "There is no condemnation to those that are in Christ-Jesus." Do you notice the word Christ-Jesus? Do you see that it is brought up into One-ness? It does not say in "Jesus" or in "The Christ"—but it says the state wherein there is no condemnation is the state of "Christ-Jesus."

The secret doctrine is beginning to ooze out of the dead letters, because at the coming of the Light within you the "graves shall give up their dead"; the graves of dead letters are releasing the glorious Truth for which we have been seeking.

The glorious winds of God have blown from you much of the old belief, and left you standing free and alone, ready to receive the adoption, to wit, the redemption of your body. Do you see that this redemption of the body is the thing that happened to Jesus, when he rose above the material concept of body and yet possessed a "Flesh and blood body"? Something to contemplate, and something that causes you to see that this resurrected or redeemed body cannot possibly come under the laws of the human belief.

You are not afraid to lose any beliefs that can be broken, for what is the good of hanging on to a belief you know may some day be broken, and pierce you? "Prove me and see" must be used with the faith that, if you prove the belief and find it without substance, that finding (however much it may upset things for the moment) will of necessity be discovered with joy. Finally the dross of human belief shall be burned out by this great honesty. You seek the Truth, and nothing but the Truth, and you do not want to fool yourself any longer with words. Either *it is* the Truth and provable as God has said, or else it is a belief that only worked in the imagination.

"I go to prepare a place for you." Already this

glorious I Am is making ready the place—is shaping it into form, as it were, so that it can come into manifestation. It is the *upper chamber* that is being made ready. The wedding of body and soul—the completeness, wholeness, and reason for being and all that which we have sought so long.

"I will never leave you," and yet "If I go I shall come again and receive you unto Myself."

You are standing before the gates of the City Beautiful, knocking upon the terrible and glorious doors. Your stand is no longer that of a beggar and outcast seeking admittance to a place which is not yours. You are knocking at the doors of your own Kingdom of Heaven. "Having done all, stand and see the salvation." See these doors swing open. You want the *Truth*, not more beautiful words and theories, and stories. You want the Truth—the reason of your existence. You want the power which belongs to you. You want the manifestation in the flesh, and you are surely going to get it when you "Stand." You are going to accept nothing less than this Power.

"Search the Scriptures, for in them ye think ye have life eternal." Remember that there is also a state that follows the "Searching and seeking," and that is the "Finding and attaining."

"*Claim your right and press your claim.*" Do you hear? I did not say get a crowd of people to do this. I said "Claim your right and press your claim." It is wonderful, for the more *your* "Claim" comes into manifestation, the more it will show a light to those who are struggling in the darkness of human belief. The command is still good—"Let your Light so shine." There is nothing yet which says you have to "make" it take place. "Press your claim" does not carry any idea of forcing. It is most nearly outpictured in the idea of hydraulic pressure. So slight on the surface of the water and yet so terrific in effect.

"And an highway shall be there, and a way, and it shall be called the way of holiness (wholeness). The unclean shall not pass over it; but it shall be for those: the wayfaring men, though fools, shall not err therein."

Have you ever wondered about all the manifestations you saw about you? Are there many things that you have to draw the curtain in front of because they cannot be explained? Yes, but do you note that in this "Highway of Wholeness" none of these things will exist. You will be raised to a level that will not be conscious of those things, and those beliefs cannot come into manifestation in this Highway of Wholeness. "But it shall be for those: The Wayfaring Men." How wonderful! The Wayfaring men usually travel alone. Do you begin to see how the dead letter is giving up its spirit, and how you are told in this beautiful secret manner about the way of Oneness? You cannot take anyone with you on this Highway of Wholeness, but just as soon as you are on it you will find thousands already travelling that same way. Yea! it is wonderful, do not fret and worry. "I have many things to say to you when you are 'wayfaring.'" Be still. The old beliefs are being swept away to make a clean place for that which transcends belief, and comes under the head of Recognition and acceptance.

The engineer who is working out glorious projects with gigantic tools and materials may sometimes smile at the child who cried over the broken toy, or the engine that was taken away from him. Do not worry —"God shall wipe all tears away," with the understanding that what you are crying over is being replaced with something so infinitely more real and True, that there is no comparison possible. So the toys of belief and system, and creed and teachers and books, and all that you will give up, will be replaced with that something which is so wonderful, that you will not be able to make any comparison. Are you afraid? Are you afraid to walk alone with this Christ? Not walking alone with an imaginary Christ, but actually to walk ALONE with your Christ? Are you afraid to have the rags of human belief stripped from you? The rags of pride, bigotry, envy, spiritual power (so called) taken from you? Instead of this mantle of personality you will be given the robe of Light and the glorious garments of attainment. Have no fear, you will not be given these robes in order that you may parade before a group of people, like a peacock, and say, "Look at me and what I have done." These robes will be given you when you are ready to receive them, and when the show of them will be the last idea.

In speaking further of this "Highway of Wholeness" we are told:

"No lion shall be there, nor any ravenous beast (the strong beliefs in powers apart from God) shall go thereon; it shall not be found there, but the redeemed shall walk there."

And what do you suppose the "Redeemed" are going to do? Just walk up and down on this highway all day long? Some people have that idea of heaven. Gradually all these stupid pictures, that have been engendered in the lives of men by the old Masters of religious paintings and stories, are passing away in favour of a glorious place of attainment. "Yes, but I cannot see what we would do if every one were perfect. Don't you think it would be monotonous?"

Of course we do not see—because we have nothing to see with, or at least that thing which sees with the understanding has not been yet put into use. The limited three-dimensional world, which is built upon contrast and pairs of opposites, does not understand the idea of "Pure joy—or perfect peace" without having its counterpart of evil. But have you ever imagined there might be a dimension of understanding which you have not yet attained, which would understand Perfection and find anything short of perfection impossible? You do not have to worry; when you are ready, the place, the understanding, and the manifestation will all come into visibility.

Do not try to grow—and do not hurry the process. "Patience must have her perfect work," and that does not mean that you are a sluggard and a dullard without interest. It means that you are standing on tiptoe of glorious aware-ness.

"And the ransomed of the Lord shall return, and come to Zion with songs and everlasting joy upon their heads; they shall obtain joy and gladness, and sorrow and sighing shall flee away."

Do you hear? You who read. I think perhaps there are many who have done away with "sorrow" in the broadest sense of the word. But is the "sighing"—that thing which is twin to "futility"—gone? Well, that seeming state which says at times, when it is tired of waiting or when its cherished beliefs are taken away, "Oh, what's the good of anything," that will be dissipated too. It shall flee away. Do you hear?

"The ransomed of the Lord" does not bespeak of the sad-faced souls that one contacts from time to time, who say they are consecrated. It will be the joyous life-giving band of people who can "Make a glad sound," and who believe in the Power of God Here and Now. It is wonderful! That "Holier than thou" attitude of mind will never find this glorious highway. Remember the prodigal was not dragged into a place of great sorrow but of great joy. All the sad-faced people who might have wanted to mourn over his shortcomings were wiped out of the picture, through the joy of the Father on receiving the Son. What is all this lofty forgiving of sin that some people do, while under their vestments they are for ever turning it over in their minds? Sin going to be discovered in the only place it ever existed, in the minds of those who are in the business of that sort of thing.

Arise! leave the filth of human belief and go to your Father. Now, do not mind what anyone says. "Salute no man as you go along the way," the Father is waiting for you. The Soul of you is waiting to reclaim the prodigal body, and make it whole and throw over it the robes of eternity. There is in reality no forgiveness in that sense of the word—there is such a glorious overshadowing of the Omnipotence of God that all is wiped out.

Do not be disillusioned, we have all been in the pigsty either physically or mentally—there is no difference. The main idea is to "Rise and go to the Father." There is going to be great rejoicing over you when you arrive—for you know there is more rejoicing over one sinner than all else. Now you can be honest with yourself.

Most of all the things in the Bible, I love those little hidden bits, that we are so prone to pass over. The infinite ways Spirit has of telling us the same thing. The infinite means it has of bringing to us that glorious state of the Here and the Now. "I speak all languages"—that is, I speak in the symbology, or signs, or words, that all can understand.

"In the habitation of dragons, where each lay, shall be grass with reeds and rushes." Do you thrill with the Life-giving energy that comes from "Then shall the lame man leap as an hart"? Have you ever surprised a deer in the forest, and seen it lift its beautiful, graceful body off the ground, and like a swiftly shot arrow divide the soft green of the forest and disappear? It is to be quickened a little, to see a thing like that. It is wonderful! Imagine the lame man leaping. Imagine him coming into one-ness with that great energy.

Can you see the hart dashing away up the side of the mountain, and jumping with infinite grace and ease from one crag to another? Do you see? You who read? Can you imagine the desert, dry and parched, suddenly bursting into bloom? Riots of colour, masses of foliage, birds dipping and skimming about, butterflies dancing in their staccato movement. Do you begin to see? This new and wonderful sense of Universal Life of which we have been talking?

Do you see, when you have conceived this holiness of Life into expression and attainment, how you cannot help shouting to the world in words and deeds, the glory of being alive?

How can you refrain from saying to them that are of fearful heart, "Be strong, fear not. Your God will come with a vengeance." Everything is all right—everything is glorious.

"Then shall the eyes of the blind be opened and the ears of the dumb unstopped," because the energy of your new Living song of Reality will burst the fetters that have bound them, and free them, too, into the glorious Recognition of that which already is. The "eyes of the blind"—your eyes, my eyes—everybody's eyes—"shall be opened"—opened to the God-world Here and Now, and ready for instant possession. "Glory to God in the Highest." The dumb shall break forth in song. And sighing and sorrow shall flee away, for the mouth of the Lord hath spoken it.

CLOTHED IN YOUR FATHER'S MIND

"So EVER-CLOTHED in your Father's Mind in the Great Omnipotent, Omniscient Spirit, in the Omniluscience of his Light, you may stand a Living Tree, and the Leaves of that Tree are for the healing of the nations, and the branches of that tree spread throughout the Universe, uniting all in One and One in All, in Life, Health and Love. For this is the New Heaven and the New Earth, the Holy City, the New Jerusalem."

"For behold the tabernacle of God is with men, and He will dwell with them, and they shall be His people, and God Himself shall be with them and be their God."

You are clothed spiritually, and as soon as you know this and accept it, you will understand how it is that "in your flesh shall you see God." You are clothed in the Mind of Your Father. You are one with Him, and He lives and moves and has His being in you at the same time you are living, breathing and having your being in Him. Thus you see the relation of Jesus-Christ and God. "I and My Father are one," "My Father is greater than I." The great essential point is that you are of one essence and substance,

171

and this entitles you to say with Jesus Christ: "All that the Father hath is mine."

When you accept the good that is yours, without discussion, without anxiety, without prying into the method of attainment, then you will begin to experience things you formerly called demonstrations, with such regularity that the heart of you will sing a lovely *new* silent-audible song. It is wonderful! Everything is all right with you. Do you hear? You, the reader of this very line. I said "Everything is all right," and there is just as much power in that statement, if accepted, as any other. When Jesus said "Stretch forth your hand," it had to be instantly accepted before it coudl be done. In some places He did not many mighty works, because they would not accept their gift. Do you hear? Suppose the man who had been commanded to "stretch forth his hand," had decided to talk it over with another, would he have ever been healed? No! because he would have fallen under the ban of human scepticism. The scales shall finally fall from your eyes, and you will learn that I AM the VOICE and I speak to you through any channel. I AM always saying "yes, you can," but so often you do not Recognize Me, because I have on no fine linen and purple. "Oh Jerusalem, Jerusalem." No! Jerusalem could not see how the carpenter of Nazareth could possibly take the City under his wing, so to speak, and he could not. Do you not see, Beloved, how many times you have missed ME, because you have looked at the garb I was wearing, instead of hearing the Voice that was giving you the command? It is wonderful! "My sheep hear my voice." Presently you are going to accept your good, no matter from what source it comes. Water through an iron pipe is just as pure and good as that which flows through a golden one. Do you hear? Do you see? "Watch, Watch, Watch"—if I speak to you on the highway, I may have something to tell you that no teacher or book says. It is wonderful!

How often have I found you at the well of life trying to draw waters, and when you drank thereof you immediately thirsted again. How often have you refused the Waters of Life I offered you. "If thou knewest the gift of God, and who it is that saith to thee, Give me to drink, thou wouldst have asked of him and he would have given thee living Waters." Do you hear? I speak to you directly. Are you thirsty? then why do you not drink of the Living Waters? The proverbial woman at the well, when asked to drink, begins to argue. She is not going to accept a gift, although it does not cost her a sou. "How could I—I have no bucket to draw the water with, and the well is deep," etc., etc. When are you going to *see* and *know* that when a thing is offered you, it is for you, and the ways and means of getting it to you will take care of themselves? Do you hear? Be sure you do, for presently I shall meet you at the well. You will be coming for Water—for some material thing. Be sure you do not miss Me again. It is wonderful! When you can stop looking for a sign, and accept unconditionally the good that belongs to the Son of the Living God, *then* you will learn something that all the people in the world cannot teach you.

"Ye did run well, who did hinder ye that you should not obey the Truth?" What was it blocked the way for you? You, who made such a flying start? It was simply that you hindered yourself by leaving the straight and narrow path of Recognition of the Presence, and straying after strange man-made gods, who had personal systems of teaching and who wanted personal followers and worshippers. Never mind, it is wonderful for you to find that "your Father has enough and to spare, no matter where this finds you."

"For you are quickened and in Spiritual, Physical and Mental radiation you are the Receiver of My Presence, and in the Realm of the Present Reign, you can truthfully and freely say, My Father and I have come to make My Abode with you. It is wonderful. Thus in your silent lectures, as well as your audible lectures, the Truth of Infinite Perfection, being modelled, moulded and shaped in the dazzling radiance and purity, shall bring forth the unity of Body, Mind and Soul. The Instantaneous transmutation of the grosser substance shall take place and shall be inevitable. It is wonderful! Your silent lectures that so many hear with the silent hearing."

Do you begin to see that the silent word, which healed the servant of the Centurion, is the word which you speak in full Recognition of your power? And you cannot do this until you accept yourself as the Son of the Living God, for who could imagine that the spoken or silent word of a little personality would amount to anything? You are beginning to accept your power, your good—yea, your heritage as the Child of the Living God.

Speak your silent word, and let the dazzling radiance of Spirit be the light which will light it into manifestation. Do not be afraid. Either the words of the Master are true or they are false. If they are true, then it is not expecting too much to see them into manifestation. Do you think so? And do you imagine that another can work them for you? Another may speak the word for you, and you may accept that glorious word, and find that the healing has taken place, but sooner or later you will have to regain your birth-right, and act as the one possessing the authority necessary to conduct this magnificient voyage upon which you are now setting out.

"You are indeed re-born—you are all made new . . . born of the Living Waters, awakened to your true, your real identity. Blessings, Blessings, Blessings. 'The Spirit and the Bride say, Come' . . . the world is preparing for the Bridegroom . . . they have heard the call and are tuning in on this great Love. It is the Allness of God and the nothingness of matter. You are hidden completely in the Secret Chamber of Christ, so submerged in the Word of This beautiful understanding and Light, that the Radiation is heard and seen and felt in the Silent Transmutation, in the Silent lectures that you so lovingly and enthusiastically speak. It is wonderful."

Do you hear? You are *re-born*—you are made anew. And the whole universe is waiting for the coming of this new-born. Waiting for the word that you will speak—the word of freedom and light, the word that you utter in the silence. "It is by My Spirit, saith the Lord"—it is not by might or by power, but by my Spirit.

"You are free. Personality may meet you, but it

can never defeat you. For you are under the Reins of
your Father, Who is ever with you, guiding you gen-
tly away from the appearances, and behold for ever the
Vision of Eternity, for I AM in you and you are in
Me. The Father and Son are One. The Rock remains
unmoved as the Prophecies unfold, for God your
Father is in authority. You are a rhapsody of Light
that outshines the Sun, in this Newness of Life."

You are free—do you see that personality may
meet you with its atrocious claims, that it is something or somebody or some power, but it will never
again defeat you. You know who you are, and you
will go silently by the way they know not of. For you
are now under the guidance of this Power within,
which is called wonderful, and upon whose shoulders
is the government. It is guiding you away "gently"
from the appearances—so be not anxious to do good
or to manifest good, all "things" are passing and the
appearances are being redeemed and relegated to
their rightful place.

"The Rock of Christ-Jesus remains eternally as the
prophecies of spirit unfold to you." The promises unfold to you and become alive. All is based on the
changeless nature of God. The shifting changing
basis of human happiness gives way before the eternal
joy of Spirit—the bliss which cannot be interpreted
or translated into human terms.

"Bless the Lord, oh my Soul, and forget not all his
benefits."

"Who satisfieth thy mouth with good things, so
that thy youth is renewed like the eagle's."

The Lord in the midst of thee "shall satisfy thy mouth with good things," which in turn "will renew thy youth as the Eagle's." It is wonderful! "Not that which goeth in, but that which cometh out of him (maketh or), defileth him." Do you see how this Hidden Manna which is given you is the only thing that can possibly "restore the years that the locusts (of age and belief) have eaten"? Do you begin to see that it is possible to bring out this glorious renewed idea of life by feeding upon the hidden manna?

"Thus I speak unto you and within you; my wisdom the infinite unlimited; my peace and my Life. My increase I impute to the permeation of every atom of your being. Every sinew, vein and bone of your body. For even as I AM so are you. Death is swallowed up in Victory.

"You will indeed smite the Rock, and as it gives forth living waters, drawing life and inspiration from the Living Source, you will know that you are Blessed, and a blessing to those with whom you come in contact, for you shall never thirst nor want as you feast on the Heavenly Manna, and drink from the Pool of Life, from the Well of Salvation that never Runs Dry.

"As long as you are lost in My will, you shall continue to ever draw greater and greater inspiration and understanding from the Living Source of all; from that Spiritual State of consciousness and understanding, from which all Reality flows into being. It is wonderful.

"You are enshrouded in My Love."

Are you afraid to rise to the occasion that confronts you, and draw from this infinite Well of Salvation all the Living Waters that are required to water the flocks that are thirsty? Are you afraid to speak the word audibly or silently, and believe in the word, and know that it is "Not by might nor by power, but by My Spirit, saith the Lord." It is wonderful when you can accept your God-given authority and utilize it out into manifestation. "Praise the Lord, oh! my Soul." The thanksgiving for this wonderful power which has come unto you, opens wider and wider the channels, so that it can flow into expression. And isn't it wonderful, now that the power is always pouring through you into expression? You will finally see that you cannot use the power too much or too often, because it will be your actual life, and the two shall be made one. Whatever you say carries the glorious silent power with it. No matter what the word is. The tone of the Voice shall awaken remembrance of the Father within the one listening or overhearing You speak. Are you afraid to accept this Voice of God? Are you afraid to admit that "God walks in you and talks in you"? Are you afraid to accept your God-given heritage? YOU I mean, not someone else—you, the one reading this line, right Now. Your God-given Freedom.

"The People of God are a peculiar people." They are peculiar because they are of God and are BELIEVERS in God. Those who truly BELIEVE in God, RECOGNIZE HIM in everything and everywhere. They believe in Jesus-Christ and his doctrine of Heaven being here and now, in counter-distinction to those who believe in Him, and yet have to wait for the fulfillment of these glorious words, or who believe that they, the poor little personalities, will have to demonstrate heaven, and perhaps share it with another. *"Take all you want but be sure you get the best."* I am speaking to you. I said *"Take all you want but be sure and take the best."* That was said to you who are reading this line. I do not know what your teacher is going to think about it. I do not know what your friend is going to say, I do not care. I do not know whether you are going to accept it or lay it aside, but I *do* know this, that it has been presented to you for your own consumption and use, and no one can use it for you. Be still and know. Just be still—I have much to say to you. You will begin the instantaneous process of accepting your good, of Recognizing your True Self, and finally of acting in this manner.

"Behold My eye is ever ON THEE, and I watch thee ceaselessly. Turn on the Light of Understanding, and in the Assurance of My Love, in the blessedness of My Ever Presence, I will Guide you and lead you through Time. I will light up your Path, and fill your heart with rejoicing and gladness and praise. Blessed indeed and a blessing to all those with whom you come in contact. For I have heard thy power before it was spoken into expression, so lift up thine eyes to the glory of Love, and you shall be filled and thrilled with the Peace of Heaven, and thou shall see clearly indeed the Infinite Blessings that I have in the storehouse for thee—yes, for thee and for all the children of men.

"Falter not, fear not, but rejoice; sing the song of Recognition as you tune in on the High vibrations of My Spirit and Love.

"I offer you good pastures and the bounties of My Love, so go forth into all the world and preach the gospel to every creature, free without purse, without scrip, and I will put My words in your mouth. I will put My spirit upon you, and I will guide you and fill you with vigour and Life eternal."

The Spirit is writing this to you through me. It is wonderful that I could say all these things to you, and that you could possess them. It is wonderful that the time has come again when you will hear the voice and live in this New Day, or close your ears to the glorious New Light and die with the old ideas and words.

"Arise and shine for thy light has come." Do not falter, do not fear. "The Lord He goeth before you and maketh straight the way." "I Am the light, the truth and the way." When you are ready to Recognize this Presence, then you can go and preach the Gospel, and take no thought of the how's and the why's. But if you think to cheat this beautiful power, and go out hoping to commercialize it, then you shall find yourself far from home without any of the needful things.

"You are indeed a blessing to all with whom you come in contact." "Blessed shall be thy going-out and thy coming in! Blessed shall thou be in the fields! Blessed shall thou be in the city! Blessed shall thou be whithersoever thou goest." Do you accept this Bless-

ing—do you carry it with you, not as some badge of honour, but as a natural emanation of the Spirit of God within you? So many blessings you cannot count them, and pretty soon they are so natural and so unexpected they happen without the slightest effort or slightest stir on your part. "Before they ask I shall answer, and while they are yet speaking I shall give it unto them."

Behold the New Day breaketh, the shadows are fleeing away—the shadows of trying to make things happen; the shadows of trying to attain the Kingdom of Heaven in some other way than that laid down by the Master. Yea, the shadows of this limited personality, that was constantly under the condemnation of your past limitations.

Arise! Son of the Living God—you are free. Free your beautiful body from the fitful limitations you have put upon it. Your Temple is a fit dwelling place for the Power of God when you Recognize the Presence and stop discounting yourself. You are as fit a receptacle for the Power of this glorious Spirit as any other Child of the Living God. Do not wait longer to claim your Birthright. Retake again that Birthright that you sold for a "Mess of pottage." You are the heir, and you are one with the Father when you Recognize the Presence and identify yourself with HIM.

"Then shall the eyes of the blind be opened and the ears of the deaf unstopped." The *then* that we have been talking about is the *Now* of Recognition. "Then shall the lame man leap as an hart." The "then" we have so long been talking about has at last become

the Now of the New Day! The doors of YOUR kingdom stand wide open to you—Child of the Living
God—the scales have dropped from your eyes—the
eyes of the Blind now SEE the LIGHT of the New
Day, and the lips of the DUMB now sing the glorious
song. It is wonderful!

LIFE

"I came that ye might have LIFE . . ." That you might have WHAT?—It says LIFE, It does not say health and something else—but LIFE—the ONE—the substance of God—in which you have your being. What then can be the matter with you—that moving and breathing and having your being in LIFE seems to manifest all sorts of things contrary to Life?

What is this "thing" in the body which is an apparent dividing line between you and life? A personal sense of life called health or disease?—A mental concept of a divided God? How can you enter into or come out of ONE? How can you have something of your *own*—a manifestation of LIFE independent of the ONE? Is it possible for you with all your mighty knowledge to divide or separate God into portions wrapped up in matter? Some good, some very good and some not so good, and some terrible?

It says nothing but evil can be gained by taking thought.—That must be the answer. You must be taking thought and that thought has formed a veil through which you attempt to force God or LIFE. It comes out evilly marked and filled with the beliefs you have picked up through the belief that you were born of a woman—instead of being projected by God.

183

LIFE is changeless and not subject to man-made laws; it is infinite and eternal. When you begin to know "ME"—then you stop knowing "me" and you find ME, LIFE—LIFE eternal. No one believes it but the one who believes it and then he BELIEVES it, and *something* begins to take place in a natural way. Limitations and beliefs disintegrate. "Whereas before I was blind"—NOW—the past and future are merged into the NOW—the substance that existed when the Angels sang together and you emerged complete and perfect, a manifestation or projection of God for the purpose of His infinite love and capacities.—Now, suddenly unsullied LIFE is flowing through you and everything, and you move and have your being in it. It is natural and normal, not something held in place by words or affirmation. It is something you could not possibly demonstrate, for it already is: It must be discovered—recognized.

"This"—this very thing you are experiencing—"IS" —(not shall be) "LIFE eternal"—the unbroken power or presence of God, flowing and flowing through the temple of you. The temple begins to be cleansed and refreshed and in some peculiar way revealed. You suddenly discover that which is within the chrysalis of the grub *belief* you have held.

And then suddenly torrents of new words—words that you have heard for aeons of time come into reality.—New words that no one believes. They pretend they believe. Suddenly you begin to get the feel of believing them. Place the coal of fire on your lips!— There is "transformation"—no one has seen it, because no one has believed. No one is going to stop you NOW from believing, and presently experiencing deep stirring within. Something will begin to show forth and after a while it seems as though it had always been that way; the former things have passed; every thing is discovered as NEW and whole and perfect. You can say "It is wonderful" if you feel like it —but don't say it just to be saying it, for nothing happens until you can say it because you cannot help saying it. "All things" and that includes you "are made new" and perfect; they are revealed in their primal state; are discovered the way they always were—and you are moving in and through and about LIFE, and you have forgotten what it feels like to know health and disease. The flow of the substance continues.

That is what "I came" for—that you might have the precious substance which cannot be affected by time, age, disease or thought—but which remains eternally as it IS. "I came that ye might have" that very substance, and that you might have more and more of it until you have had an abundance of it—an abundance of LIFE here and there and everywhere, even in Hell, and watch it come into being in perfection and beauty.

I don't care with what swine of belief you have been associating—I do not care if you are covered with the mud of belief and are searching for a grain of wheat in the chaff of human teaching—I know that the moment you REMEMBER, the purifying fires will be lighted. That is what I came for. It is wonderful!

HELPING OTHERS

"To LIFT a soul above its *natural* level is a dangerous act, for when the soul is forced upwards and then seeks its own level again, it disintegrates."

"To the poor the gospel is preached. . . ." The *poor* are not only those without money; they are those who are poor mentally, physically, and spiritually. The "treatment" is the same in all cases.

Jesus helped millions—and is still helping them. But one thing was always required—and that was RECOGNITION. Unless the Power was recognized, embodied in the flesh, He could do nothing. It is recorded that in some places He did not many mighty works because of the failure to *recognize* the Power— the WORD MADE FLESH.

So often we rush in where angels fear to tread, taking over the problem instead of *revealing* the Gospel —the revelation that would *lift* the needy one to a level in which he could help himself. The moment we descend to the level of the person we are trying to help, we can do nothing—and this we do when we recognize his condition as needing *our* help. You do not go to the bottom of the well to rescue the one who has fallen in.

187

You cannot fill a barrel that has a hole in it—neither can you fill a human mind with the consciousness of God if that mind is still considering his problem as a reality. YOU can *try* to help another by descending to his level through sympathy,—and presently, like a beetle in a slippery bowl, you arrive at his level, and get in his way. Your efforts become as nothing, and you find yourself trampled beneath the feet of a greedy, ungrateful human mind that wants things done on the outside. Then *you* begin the old ditty about "ingratitude."

Anything or anybody with whom you sympathize has a stranglehold on you and will finally take you to his level—and you will not like it. Jesus had no *sympathy* with anything—but He had infinite compassion that would forgive seventy times seventy. Forgiving is not condoning—and "turning the other cheek" is not weakness or an acknowledgment of defeat.

Sooner or later you will discover that your best efforts to help have failed—your good deeds have been charged off as nothing—and you have made an enemy.

If we would only remember the "Such as I have"—instead of tossing golden coins into the lap of the beggar. They only prolong the day of wrath for him—whereas the "Such as I have" might cause him to end the evil picture, and renew his strength and gratitude. Yet would you literally give your all?

Jesus certainly did not withhold when He gave bread and fish to the hungry men. "*They* followed Him into a desert place." He did not force them to go. Then they began to *murmur*—and what a *murmur five thousand men* could make, not to mention the *women* and *children* and *dogs*. Yes, it must have been quite a *murmur*, if you see what I mean. He fed them *once*—and what happened? The hole in the barrel was not stopped, and the next morning they were back again for more bread. And then He rebuked them, saying, "What? Did ye not see the miracle?" If they had, that *would* have stopped up the hole (or lack) in consciousness. They were so engrossed with *things*, they had no time for that. And then to make it more emphatic that He was not going to give more bread, He said, "Children, have you any meat?" I am sure it was with humor that He brought home this lesson.

No, they did not see the *miracle*—just the manifestation. What are *you* looking for?

Had they been able to SEE the miracle, they would have known the technique of bringing bread into manifestation, literally as well as symbolically. What would have happened if Jesus had continued to give them bread? Soon whatever gratitude they may have had would have turned into jealousy.

"For what I would, that do I not, but what I hate, that I do." And you have hurt those you wanted most to help. Many times the one you have lifted up temporarily disintegrates or goes back to his former state, cursing you. This is as it should be. Next time you will recognize his soul instead of his sense.

Every *concession* you make to an evil weakens the sum total of your ability to help. And yet with what overflowing love Jesus gave the "miracle," the technique of healing, to *anyone* who would come and eat and drink without price; and so will you do likewise.

Another interesting point is that Jesus would listen

to *no* arguments or speculations of evil—neither did he believe in *post-mortems*. Speculation on the outcome of a problem or evil that might happen is a *sure way* to experience *that* evil. And this goes for speculation on another's problem, too.

"To him that hath shall it be given." Hath what? Hath *consciousness*—for he knows that "If I be lifted up from the earth (to a higher state of consciousness) I will draw all men (manifestation on that level) to ME." If he can be lifted up to the *recognition* that God is "no respecter of persons" but gives to *any* man who will *take*, then he has received riches beyond the gold of Ophir. Then he has the pearl of great price which no man can take from him. He who will preach this gospel will merge into a NEW STATE wherein he will feel the rich, magnificent, reciprocal integration of God taking place.

Yes—but there are *only* three drops of oil—I have nothing with which to start! The command "Start pouring" has to be accepted and acted upon, else you will continue to have but three drops. At the first movement of the power, start praising and glorifying it. Keep your attention away from the empty measures all about you, presently you will have to "borrow measures not a few." It will keep flowing, once you start praising and recognizing it and have taken your attention away from what *ought* to be done.

Few great fortunes have been started with large sums of money. Most of them started from the handful of meal and the three drops of oil. Why? Because working from the outside causes the whole picture to collapse. There is nothing within to support it. A handful of snow started down the mountainside becomes the avalanche in the valley. And so it is with you.

Do not make the mistake of being caught in the bramblebush of self-pity. Do not say, "Look what I did for him, and what happened." Forget it—bless him and his on-going—and presently he will see the LIGHT and beat a new path to your heart and lay his gift on the altar.

After you have made the mistake of helping in the wrong way, do not condemn yourself. If you recognize it, that is enough. Bless everything and love everything, pouring floods of love over it all. Love is the one gift that NEVER FAILETH. It is wonderful!

JESUS AND THE LEPERS

As JESUS *passed* through a *small* village, ten lepers called to him—and He healed them and went on His way. The effortlessness of this mass healing is astounding, since today when we hear of a person being cured of leprosy, it makes the headlines. With what Divine indifference He did this apparent miracle!

What happened from the moment the leper asked to be made clean and the answer of Jesus when He said, "I will; be thou clean!" Something tremendous —and yet nothing, for it was already established in the Mind of God. The *action* took place in *human mind*. When the change took place, the congested atoms of thought which formed the evil picture gave way and the perfect manifestation came to light again.

So it is wonderful,when we see the Divine indifference with which HE let the Power of God manifest on the earth—at no time giving a degree of intensity to the thing called evil. There was not something that was worse than something else—it was all from the same cause, a belief in two powers.

When we think of the ten men who were healed, we wonder what their thoughts were. If, as we hear today, a given disease is caused by a given thought, did all these men have a common thought?

193

Throughout the New Testament we see the *Divine indifference* of Jesus—and the lavishness of His giving, as in the case of the five thousand loaves and fishes. We also see a *Divine integrity*—"Gather up the fragments that remain, that NOTHING BE LOST." This shows a very essential LAW in the life of Jesus —and something very necessary in the life of man, opening a vista of the why of it all. The carelessness of many people is imagined to be Divine indifference —but there is a great discrepancy between the two.

So we hear Jesus speaking the few words, "I will; be thou clean," wiping out the picture which, from a human standpoint, originated from all sorts of causes: i.e., heredity, environment, and false teaching.

But stay a moment, I pray thee—we find Him asking, "Where are the other nine?" Why did He care? What difference did it make? The *Divine indifference* has its echo in *Divine integrity*. Jesus knew that the other nine had gone back to get more leprosy—for they had not made the final acknowledgment. In a little while, consorting again with *the man whose breath was in his nostril*, they would reproduce the picture which had been dispelled. Yes, the Divine indifference, which appears so careless in its manner, is Divine *order* fundamentally.

> "*Consider* the lilies of the field, how they grow;
> they toil not, neither do they spin, and yet . . .

Many seekers for things and ideas have misunderstood these words, trying to operate them for money. When you *consider* the lilies, you are amazed to see what takes place. And when you *do* see this, you will know that "they toil not" because they develop

effortlessly through the *Love of God* and the LIFE,
which is eternally spontaneous and makes no duplicate
manifestations. *You* are also that individualized manifestation of God; there is not another like you. This
is the password to success, for it takes you directly
into the field of *no competition*—and automatically
you feel the success of "they toil not" coming into
expression. Do you SEE?

Isn't it interesting that the ten lepers were in a
small village. There is so much evil where the consciousness is small. How prolific the evil of the *little
human* thought can be? Do you begin to see?

Do you understand how it is that the Lord has
provided the *Cities of Refuge*—a sanctuary of protection—into which you may run at any moment and feel
the refreshing Presence of Spirit. Can you imagine
running into the cool quiet of the temple with its
beautiful subdued light—the faint notes of the organ
clinging, like slowly moving doves, about the altar.
"But NOW, at this moment of recognition, the Lord,
your God, hath given you rest on EVERY side—
(do you hear what it says?)—so that there is neither
adversity nor evil occurrent."

Literal interpretation killeth the *words* of Jesus, for
there is no *light* in them. They may be angelic words,
but truly as sounding brass and tinkling cymbals—no
healing, no power. It is strange how quickly, when
the WORD is in the *words*, the sudden coming of
power and change takes place. When Pluto released
Persephone from the infernal regions, Ceres cele-
brated with the Festival of Spring. You can experience
the JOY OF SPRING symbolically, and literally—
the thrill of trees bursting into bloom, green grass

shooting up everywhere, birds darting about, singing —the ploughman joyously tracing the warm dark furrows—life and life more abundantly—all this is vaguely suggestive of what takes place in you when you even think of the *WORD* Jesus Christ.

Do you know how it is that with the coming of this WORD in you, you lose your limited sense of Life and are *blended* with the ONE LIFE, like the drop of dirty water that at last tumbles into the sea and is purified? At *this very instant in the body-temple, you are experiencing the transformation and the reincarnation*. The atoms are reassembled, as were those in the body of the leper. And lo! you are transformed—RE-FORMED—made NEW—*reincarnated in the flesh!*

There is the place of "touch me not." The things that had to do with the former incarnation are of no avail in the new. As grotesque as it may seem to the human reason, the final step will be made and man will *reincarnate* in the present body, changing it until "they (the former witnesses to your limitations) shall know thee no more." It is wonderful to contemplate this when it is kept on the basis of intense practicality and does not become mere imagination and the stuff of dreams.

UNTRAMMELED ACTION

WHEN YOU, through recognition, touch the Truth, suddenly you *live*—for automatically you enter a new mansion, degree or dimension of life. Universal consciousness it a huge honeycomb. There are endless degrees—endless on-goings into higher and greater elevations of Light—always finding it becomes increasingly simple as you merge more completely into the ONE, the infinite.

Healing, which was considered miraculous formerly, is only Recognition—not in any way manipulated by taking thought or by handling thought patterns. Discovery and recognition of the Permanent Identity causes it to rise to the surface like a cork which has been held under water and suddenly released. It leaves far behind all thought of creation or re-creation—and stands in the flooding light of revelation. "Behold I make *all* things new." The "I" which is the Permanent Identity—the Christ within you—when it appears, reveals everything new and changed. The former things can no longer hold on. Like beetles trying in vain to hold on to the surface of a crystal globe, so do the former beliefs and diseases slip off into oblivion. "Behold" is a state of "breathless adoration"—or pure recognition. It automatically takes

197

place. The *golden being* appears on the surface of human beliefs. You stand in the eternal ways of Life. All this, which is so difficult to record, is as simple and natural as the coming of dawn. That is why the "Kingdom of Heaven is given unto the Child"—consciousness—the consciousness which can accept realities instead of trying to reason them out. "Who then by taking thought?" The more you *think* about it, the more impossible it becomes, and the deeper you sink into the mire of human belief which coagulates and sets about you like cement. There is no escape through thought.

"But when He shall appear"—we shall be LIKE Him, for we shall see *Him* as He is. We shall discover that permanent being in the midst of the confusion of human thought and discover what He is like. The holy purpose of your appearing shall be made manifest.

Yes, there is a reason for the hope that is within *you*—but until you dare to "Come to ME" in the wonder-BELIEF of the here and NOW, you go the lonely way of all dreamers—into the lotus land of imagination and unfulfilled wishes.

Healing then is revelation—is recognition—is the daring to call the Lazarus forth without the thought of miracle-working—but with the infinite harmony which is octaves beyond the human belief.

THE BRANCH

THE BRANCH from which was fashioned the crown of thorns which Jesus wore was once a soft bud which could have been crushed easily. So with all ugly manifestations of life—in the beginning they are nothing but the undeveloped idea or thought and could be instantly deleted and deprived of manifestation. *Instant* prayer is not a preachment of words—it is merely being on the alert to crush the thought before it has time to manifest in shape and form.

Jesus telescoped time and space not as "magic" but rather because He saw the all-over aspect of the idea. He saw the flower *before* the seed, and vice versa, since they are all one and complete in the initial creation, and not a matter of time and space. "You say it is yet four months to the harvest?" A question that can be answered but one way, "Yes," because the human intellect must go through time and space to see anything. Until man does return to the point of oneness, he cannot see the *whole*, only a part of the idea. It is so with *substance*. The seed that is held in thought dies. It must be cast into the ground—the very act is recognition. The substance *is* before the seed. All this is abstruse to human intellect; yet it can happen and has happened, but NOT by taking thought. The moment reason enters, inspiration disappears. It is something that cannot be captured by human thought or words, or yet compressed into an object. "I"—the real *I* of you—has a way that the John Smith conglomeration of ideas and beliefs of you knows not of and *never* can know, because he has not the capacity with which to do it.

ANIMAL MAGNETISM

AT THIS late date one still encounters people who fear the witchcraft of the jungle, still believing that the thoughts of another can injure them, or even kill.

One might be surprised to find that what he believes to be animal magnetism and mental malpractice is merely a bad case of egotism. I have often known people who are fearful most of the time, imagining some one was "malpracticing" on them. If they would make a check-up on themselves, they would find they have little to justify the effort of anyone. Whom do *you* know that *you* would like to keep thinking of all the time? Are you important enough for another to occupy his time with the bother of thinking about you?

Animal magnetism and malpractice were brought from the dark places of ignorance and can only operate where ignorance is present. They are often used as an excuse for failure to produce results from Truth. Many so-called *advanced souls*, gurus or masters, when they are unable to call upon their God and get results, need a subterfuge or excuse for the evil that happens and their failure to destroy it. They need a sop for their failure to recognize the Power. They take refuge in blaming their shortcomings on animal magnetism. Who is going to waste precious time thinking about you, when he could do something much nicer?'

PRE-BIRTH WISDOM

"The souls knew everything they learned on earth, prior to their coming into the world."

THESE WORDS of an ancient unknown Wise Man, verify what Jesus knew and manifested, and make possible the statement, "I can do all things through Christ Jesus." When *Jesus* went to the Father, He discovered the answer to all questions—and not only the answer, but the ability to step them down into visibility. Trying to create them in the *outside*, then, is folly—trying to demonstrate them is futile.

Faith, being both the *substance* and the *evidence* of the pre-existing state, or the *soul state* wherein all things are known, we understand that by the use of this *Faith* we pass through the darkness of human thought into the place of LIGHT and REVELA-TION—and therein find the established facts.

The question is—Why does the soul—which knows everything it is to learn (being endowed with all knowledge and ability), apparently lose this capacity when it enters into manifestation and why does it have to be *instructed* to remember?

The answer is that when spirit is stepped down to a point of visibility (called matter, a body for the soul), the soul moves into a new medium, in which perception is practically nil—and in order to regain this perception much learning is employed. Once, however, the soul discovers the Permanent Identity and its capacity, it will bring what it discovers into full-fledged manifestation. "I can do all things through Christ Jesus" is then a definite orientation into a world of power—a point where *discovery* of *established wisdom* is reached. The desires of the human mind are seen as the *coming events* which cast their shadows before them.

Once it is accepted that the *soul* knows everything it *tries* to learn on earth, it will appropriate a dimension of wisdom equal to that understanding. This cannot be *demonstrated* by the curious human mind which thinks to *try* it. It is either accepted and experienced, or discussed in the jungle of human ideas.

It is possible to hold a book in your hands, with the acceptance of your *birthright*, and know the contents without the labor of reading it line for line. A cursory glance at its pages will verify this fact, but if you were foolish enough to attempt to show this to the profane, you would only succeed in making yourself a laughing-stock. "Cast not your pearls before swine." None of this is for the purpose of working wonders—nor yet for the idea of making money. The deceived mind that approaches it with the gluttony of the human thought is turned awry, or returns to his *positive knowledge* that it doesn't work—and it doesn't. But IT DOES!

If I *had* only the words of an ancient Wise Man for this magnificent LAW, I would have small assurance indeed—but when the LIVING, BREATH-

ING, LUMINOUS CONSCIOUSNESS of Jesus
Christ verified it in a thousand and one ways, I feel
safe in walking on the waters of human disbelief and
seeing this quality of HIS LOVE come true. The
soul that has contacted Jesus Christ is *unafraid* to
follow His commandments. *The timid soul sinks by
its own fear.* The touching of this PURE CON-
SCIOUSNESS is what produces a genius who *knows*
—but has no credentials of human learning.

Do not *try* to use this power—it is not for that
purpose. All *effort* is of the human mind. It is through
RECOGNITION of this LIGHT that an effort-
less change in the program and on-going of man
takes place. He operates from the elevation of Jesus
Christ—who turns *within*, perceives the *finished idea*
—and hears it *called from the housetop* of manifestation. The picture *shown on the Mount* casts its shadow into the realm of matter—and remains in position so long as the consciousness of it remains.

The instant you "go to the Father" you become
totally alive. The Light searches the joints and mar-
row, and a putrefying Lazarus suddenly becomes
totally alive.

A further burst of light coming from the same
Wise Man is:

"All human souls before coming down to earth
were present in the *Divine Idea*, in the same form
that they were to have in the world."

This sounds very much like the words of Jesus:

"And now, O Father, glorify thou me
with thine own self

> With the glory which I had with thee
> before the world was."

It is thrilling to contemplate this perfection which comes up through the shadow-pictures. Jesus showed *it coming through* in the transfiguration. It is indicated again in

> "Be ye transformed
> By the renewing of your mind."

Again and again the artist goes to the idea he is reproducing. And so man returns to the "picture shown him on the Mount"—discovering the capacities therein and bringing them into manifestation—not as a miracle or unnatural event, but as a very normal expression of something that already is. I can, therefore, "Do all things through Christ Jesus," whether I have learned anything about them or not. Likewise do I *know* all things, both past and future, concerning the shadow-picture. Functioning from the place of soul, I can change or disintegrate them.

The destiny of man made in the "IMAGE AND LIKENESS OF GOD" is eternally perfect and intact. When he descended into the manifest world of human thought, he forgot much, and has endeavored to recapture the dream within his soul. He has fallen under the hypnosis of *judging from appearances,* believing them to be real and a reliable source for his information. Consequently he has built up a human *fate* pattern which is largely evil, for it all comes from his human forebears and partakes of all the ensuing evils and limitations. The instant he recognizes his Divine source and destiny, things happen which the world calls miracles—but it is just the out-picturing of the Life Pattern from the standpoint of SOUL instead of from matter. He then bridges years of ignorance and is found expressing himself along lines for which he has made no preparation—for, in reality, he knows everything he has *tried to learn* on the earth-plane, before he descended to heavier planes of matter.

"I stir up your pure minds
BY WAY OF REMEMBRANCE."

We begin to grasp the idea that the *mission* of Christ is to save *Jesus* (John Smith) or to prove that manifestation can be and is lifted above the evils of human thought. Knowing, then, that "if I be lifted up, I shall draw all manifestation unto me," we discover that as we enter the realm of soul, we are lifted to the place of the finished mystery—and shall draw all things to us in freedom and harmony. We begin to understand the *contemplation* of the POWER within—and we become *lost* in LIFE, freed from the confines of *health* and its negative pole, disease.

The awakening to our *raison d'être* causes us to do a rightabout from the old treadmill of fighting against principalities and powers of darkness. We discover something is to be *accepted*, and not created. It is recorded:

"Everyone that is called of my name,
I have created in my glory,
I have formed him,
Yea, I have made him."

This is the spiritual creation which antedates the

human coming into being. It has little to do with the odious command to work out your living "by the sweat of thy brow." It takes just this recognition of the permanent quality of the SOUL, in contradistinction to the transient condition of the mask or body, to accomplish the so-called miracles. "I have created him for my glory" is enough to start a whole new routine of life, wherein swirls of unseen power are manifested in new dimensions of expression.

Consciousness is really an abstract form of thought —a point beyond thinking. It is the source from which all things of reality flow into being. "Leave all—follow ME" indicates the way. We leave all the shadows of thought and return to the SOUL, the CHRIST, which already knows everything it is trying to learn on the earth plane.

> "If any of you lack wisdom,
> Let him ask of God. . . .
> And it shall be given him."

The only place you can reach God is *within*. The daring to ask God, knowing that the Soul of you knows everything it is going to learn on earth, many times instantly sets aside all the human steps of learning, leading up to expression. "In the twinkling of an eye all shall be changed." The moment it is found as a reality in the soul, it becomes a working principle on the earth. You *know* it—you ARE it.

Jacob dreamed of the ladder extending to heaven, with angels ascending and descending. These were the *thoughts* of God passing to man, and establishing a new order and regime. So it is with you when you are ready to experience this wonder. The ladder ex-

tending from the heart of God will rest in the heart
of you when you are "asleep" (not thinking)—and
you will be filled with the HOLY GHOST.

Instantaneous demonstrations, so much cited of
yore, are merely moments when man has been able
to ascend to the Permanent Identity, and discover
the WISDOM already established there. It is not
a matter of "learning"—but of discovery.

Speaking of THE CHRIST, Paul says:

"Who is the image of the invisible God,
the first-born of all creation;
For in Him were all things created,
in the heaven and upon the earth,
Things visible and things invisible,
whether thrones, or dominions or
principalities, or powers;
All things have been created through Him,
and unto Him,
And He is before all things and in Him
all things consist."

When we contemplate *this* CHRIST, we begin to
understand the magnitude of His power and offices
toward *the Jesus.* "I can do all things through Christ"
then does not seem such a Herculean feat as formerly.
To discover the finished state is to manifest it.

Once we recognize the Christ, we see that *mani-festation* from there on depends more on the *receiver*
than the Giver—that is, the willingness and capacity
to receive the inrush of this established wisdom and
learning which has been so remote and difficult of
attainment. "Open wide the doors of the Temple"
—let the Son of Man pass through into all His Glory.

Yes, "I can do all things through Christ"—and I know all things. I can ask and receive because I am at the elevation of asking only for that which is already established. waiting to be stepped down to a point of visibility through my body-temple.

> "Elohim is the prototype of all being, and all things are in Him, in their purest and most complete form; so that the perfection of the created consists exactly in the existence, in which they find themselves (in affinity) with the original source of their being; and in proportion to the distance of their departing from the Deity, they will sink down from that perfect and sublime condition."—Cordovera, A.D. 1522.

Reflection or material concept is entirely dependent upon the *degree* to which we contemplate the prototype or perfection of the Christ within. This is not "demonstrating" God—but releasing that which is already created into a place of manifestation. The shape and form of the reflection changes as we contemplate the *perfection* within. Sometimes, in the "twinkling of an eye," when we have perceived this finished mystery, a loathsome disease disappears— evil conditions are made nil—and the former things pass away. All this is in the MIND WHICH WAS ALSO IN CHRIST JESUS—and which you are invited to "let be in you."

> "Ye shall draw water with joy
> From the wellsprings of salvation."

The "wellsprings of salvation" are found in the consciousness of Jesus Christ—and from this very place shall the WATERS OF LIFE flow freely into manifestation. The recognition of these ever-flowing wells of salvation is what makes it possible to find "wells" in the desert places and "springs" in dry lands —both literally and figuratively.

The next time you are swamped by your ignorance, *contemplate* the revelation of the Wise Man:

"The souls knew everything they learned on earth prior to their coming to the earth."

and you will discover some of the WISDOM OF GOD within you. Stop discounting your DIVINITY. Stop talking to the man whose breath is in his nostrils. Recognize your Divinity. WHO ARE YOU? Who do men say that you are? And WHO do *you* say you are?

"Know ye not your own selves,
How that Jesus Christ IS IN YOU?"

PRAYER

"I am conscious of something within me that plays before my soul, and is as a light dancing in front of it; were this brought to steadiness and perfection in me, it would surely be eternal Life. . . .—St. Augustine.

"But I think thine horse would sooner *con* an oration, than thou learn a prayer without a book."—Shakespeare.

Man has come to think of *prayer* as a formula printed in a book, or given him by some "spiritual" leader. Prayer is the *up-gush* of God in your heart. *You* do not need words with which to pray—only the fervent recognition of the PRESENCE. Words are futile and worthless—empty, and of no avail as compared to the inner recognition of the Lord and Master. *This* you can do without lessons on "How to Pray." The Master said, "When ye pray, *believe* (not with intensity) that ye receive, and it shall be so." What simplicity and how natural! *When* the Lord hath spoken within the midst of thee, then He will speak audibly through your temple so that you can *Hear* and *do*.

213

In the *revelation*, everything is a reversal of the human thought or belief. It finally reveals to man that the illusion of human creation is nothing but the pictures cast on the ethers, which are disintegrating as fast as they form. Virgil says:

"He who sings THY praise, secures his own."

He who *recognizes* THE ONE, secures his own oneness and experiences the things that are neither seen nor heard, nor yet thought of—but which are all established.

The *human mind* does not want a *healed* world. It protests that it *does*, but not being able to imagine a state of life wherein the old pair of opposites is not present, it continues to need its evil, in order to display its *good*.

A healer with office, telephone, and time on her hands, was surprised when told it was wonderful that she had no patients. Isn't that what she had been "treating" for all the time, i.e., "to know there is no evil"? Now that she had arrived at a place where no evil was brought into her presence, she should have felt successful. But she protested: "What about my telephone and office rent?"

"This above all, to thine own self be true, then it will follow. . . ." *That* is about it. Are you after the loaves and fishes or after ME? Do you imagine you can fool God while you are fooling man about your desire to do good? When you see one who is so anxious to do good, what must be the natural deduction? Are *you* anxious to do good? Why?

You can brush disease from the temple with the same ease you brush dust away. Do you hear? Are you following ME—or are you trying to? When will you, without taking thought, come to ME, disregarding all the thought patterns which make the coming utterly impossible? You CAN experience the QUICKENING *right* NOW. It is all so possible, as you are, NOW, as you read these lines, experiencing the PRESENCE as something real and tangible instead of a nebulous idea in mind. As I am recording this, you are feeling it—we are at the point of agreement—we are TOUCHING the consciousness of Jesus Christ, even as the woman in the crowd touched His consciousness and caused the virtue, or manifestation, to take place. NOW are you HEARING? Past and future are NOW. All I write in the Past and all you read in the Future are NOW—HERE in the mind of God. Do you begin to see?

"When we pray, we should open our heart to God like a fish when it sees a wave coming."—Vianney.

A day comes when the puny heartbeat, struggling against the load of thought and beliefs of a human mind, catches the heartthrob of God. From then on new LIFE, new MANIFESTATION takes place. Things transpire that are beyond explanation. The extension of the senses opens as a fan of LIGHT.

For God, who commanded the LIGHT to shine out of darkness, hath shined *in our hearts*, to give the light of knowledge of the GLORY of God in the face of Jesus Christ.
But we have this treasure in *earthen vessels*, that the excellency of the power may be of God, and not of us.

This is SECRET DOCTRINE.
Can you imagine the fierce heartbeats of Jesus

when He decided to descend to the place of thinking, and let the vicious, murderous thought of man
be loosed upon Him? From the human point of view,
the struggle must have been terrific. *Once*, for a brief
moment He thought to abandon it, but remembered
... "and he shall presently give me more than twelve
legions of angels." At that memory He knew the
moment He made His contact with the ONE, the
whole picture of human suffering would disappear.
But yet the heart of Him beat terrifically until He
again caught the throb of the heart of God and ascended in consciousness. So with you, the moment
you recognize the ONE, the puny heartbeat will
become one with the throbbing heartbeat of God,
and you will experience ONENESS with the pulsa-
tion of the universe. You will partake of some of the
things Jesus could not tell you in Jerusalem because
you were not ready to *hear* them. Now it can be told
—NOW it can be whispered into the heart of you,
and you can appropriate the gift of Jesus Christ
catching the heartthrob of God.

THEN WENT HE IN

"THEN WENT He in and *shut* the door" finally becomes something more than words. It becomes a
definite, literal action. From this elevation, the transition takes place—not the cure, not the healing; not
the patching up of old temples, but the REVELA-
TION of something entirely NEW. No more "clam-
oring with the midnight and the storm," trying to
defeat evil, or yet to establish good.

Eventually you, too, have the great *task* to under-
take, you have to meet *yourself* (John Smith), alone
and unaided. You have this to do, or be defeated by
him. It is hard to be alone with *John Smith*. Jesus was
driven to the wilderness in order that He could meet
Jesus. If you are after something more than a demonstration, which like the grass of the fields is here
today and tomorrow cast into the oven, you, too,
will have to meet John Smith finally. When you do,
something like this will happen:

A letter:
I have been enjoying the most wonderful quietness and unfoldment of the harmony and order
of the Universe. Without a book, without the

counsel of a friend, far from the influence of the crowds and the screaming protestations of the hordes of so-called Truth seekers, the mystery of Creation and my unity with its Infinite Source has been unfolding and flooding me with a light that grows brighter and brighter with each succeeding expansion of consciousness.—Maynard M.

There comes the day when the old ideas pass away —the thought-taking processes of patching up the body, curing it, trying to make it over, go. "BEHOLD, all things are made NEW" and "Ye must be born again" become statements of established laws as soon as you leave the prison, the squirrel cage of affirmations, the treatments and demonstrations, together with all the nonsense that you can in *any way* influence God. The only power you have is in aligning yourself with God.

The moment this iconoclastic revelation is seen, you experience a transition. The old superstructure begins to come down. The Temple is searched *within* and *without*. Now the "inside of the platter" is made clean, freed from the thieves of thought. You are "born again" literally. Do not become excited because of the shifting, pulling down, changing conditions in the Temple. All things are to be made or revealed as NEW and BEAUTIFUL.

The *chaos* sometimes seems worse than the former state of things. The urge to "return to Egypt" comes. But once you recognize what is going on, you will retire to the CENTER of your BEING—and *let* the storm of thought spend itself. Presently the fury will have passed—and you will emerge on a calm sea. "Be not afraid—it is I." The great transition is taking place —and it is WONDERFUL.

No man can create a body for a soul. In his conceit and blindness he may think he can, but he has no more power than had the ninety-year-old Abraham when told of the coming event. He laughed with derision. When the LOVE OF GOD (not the love of man) moves upon the face of the deep, something takes place and is formed. This is not the result of emotional ecstasy, but an outpicturing of God.

The beautiful temple of Love appearing before the human level of things is misjudged and smeared with the limitations of thought, finally dropping with age. All of this he believes to be his heritage.

When Jesus contemplated the Golden Being—the image and likeness of His being—it came to the surface. It is this *precise* recognition which takes place when a so-called healing is made. The permanent identity rises through the mask of human thought and ancestor worship.

Note: He took the disciples to a high mount—none of these wonders can be done in the cesspool of human thought and speculation, belief in magic, or at the prophecy of the necromancer who believes in signs and wonders.

"Ye must be born again" is a literal command. The recognition of this capacity causes the body to become plastic—to change *completely*.

As the old, fixed forms begin to change, many things are brought to the surface and eliminated. Do not be excited about appearances. They will change as the NEW LIFE comes to the surface and reveals to you the fair proportions of the TEMPLE BEAUTIFUL.

"Before the phantom of False Morning died, methought a VOICE within the tavern cried, 'When all the Temple is prepared within, why nods the drowsy worshipper outside?' "—Omar Khayyam.

"Go in and shut the door"—you are alone—NOW.

By Walter C. Lanyon

The Eyes of the Blind	$6.00
Without the Smell of Fire	$6.00
The Laughter of God	$6.00
The Joybringer	$4.00
The Temple Not Made With Hands	$6.00
A Light Set Upon A Hill	$6.00
London Notes and Lectures	$6.00
Thrust in the Sickle	$6.00

By Norman P. Grubb

Who Am I?	$2.50
God Unlimited	$4.50
Deep Things of God	$3.50
Yes I Am	$5.00
Spontaneous You	$3.00
Key to Everything	.50

By Union Life Ministries

Infinite Supply	$5.00
The Mystery of the Gospel	$1.50

Please add 50¢ for any order of less than $5.00. Three weeks should be allowed for delivery—orders are not sent first class mail unless specifically requested and paid for at the time of the order.

All of the above books can be ordered from:

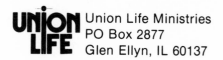 Union Life Ministries
PO Box 2877
Glen Ellyn, IL 60137